# CRACKING THE
# CURIOSITY
# CODE

D1617254

# CRACKING THE CURIOSITY CODE

## The Key to Unlocking Human Potential

### DIANE HAMILTON, PhD

gatekeeper press

Columbus, Ohio

Cracking the Curiosity Code:
The Key to Unlocking Human Potential

Published by Dr. Diane Hamilton, LLC

Copyright © 2018 by Dr. Diane Hamilton, PhD

ISBN (hardcover): 9781642373479
ISBN (paperback): 9781642373462
eISBN: 9781642373455

Printed in the United States of America

# *Dedication*

For Tom Tate, who always challenged me and inspired me to embrace my natural sense of curiosity.

*Praise for*
## *Cracking the Curiosity Code*

Among its virtues, Dr. Diane Hamilton's well-researched, highly useful and very timely book, *Cracking the Curiosity Code*, gives critical advice for how to overcome the factors that hold individuals and organizations back from achieving their full potential.

**Steve Forbes**
**Chairman and Editor-in-Chief of Forbes Media**

Diane Hamilton gives you everything you need to know on curiosity, all wrapped in a book that surely will make you a better business manager or, for that matter, parent. *Cracking the Curiosity Code* is a crackerjack book loaded with prizes.

**Ken Fisher**
**Executive Chairman, Fisher Investments**
**New York Times Bestselling Author**

Curiosity is THE foundational talent which will continue to differentiate those who lead in their field, industry, and life. Diane has created a ground-breaking book and assessment to help people overcome the things that hold them back from being curious. Just as understanding the importance of emotional intelligence has led to success, developing curiosity could foreseeably be the next movement to enhance human performance.

**Verne Harnish**
**Founder, Entrepreneurs' Organization (EO)**
**Author of *Scaling Up (Rockefeller Habits 2.0)***

In *Cracking the Curiosity Code*, Diane Hamilton not only illustrates how everything from newborns to click-bait ads harnesses our natural instinct for curiosity to succeed, but also sparks the curiosity of readers to be more inquisitive in their work and life.

**Jay Samit**
**Serial Disruptor,**
**Author of *Disrupt You!***

The cost of learning is significantly less than the cost of ignorance. Curiosity may kill the cat, as the old saying goes; but, better yet, it kills ignorance. Dr. Diane

Hamilton's latest book, *Cracking the Curiosity Code*, will certainly enhance your sense of curiosity.

**Dr. Tony Alessandra**
**Founder of Assessments24x7.com**
**Author of *People Smart in Business***

In today's turbulent world, personal curiosity leads to organizational creativity that leads to sustainable success. Diane Hamilton's brilliant and useful book reminds us that curiosity can be acquired and mastered. Her insights, tools, and examples show us how to become more curious by observing, asking questions, learning, and improving.

**Dave Ulrich**
**Rensis Likert Professor, Ross School of**
**Business, University of Michigan**
**Partner, The RBL Group**

As organizations recognize the importance of engagement, emotional intelligence, and other soft skills, developing curiosity is the one overlooked factor that significantly impacts success. Dr. Diane Hamilton's ground-breaking research explores the importance of curiosity and explains how to improve it for highly innovative workplaces where employees can make significant contributions, feel more empowered, and become aligned to what truly inspires them.

**Kevin Kruse**
**Founder and CEO of LEADx**
**New York Times Bestselling Author**

I believe one of the most powerful ways to motivate ourselves is to ask questions. When we're curious about what else we might do, how things work, and how others think, we get to live extraordinary lives. Dr. Diane Hamilton has written a phenomenal guide to our curiosity. Read it. Benefit from it. Enjoy a more fulfilling life!

**Tom Hopkins**
**Hall of Fame Speaker**
**Author of *When Buyers Say No***

*Cracking the Curiosity Code* is an eye opener. Reading self- and business-improvement books for decades, once in a while a new idea hits home as impactful, new, and important. This is one of those rare books that's worth reading. Thanks to Diane Hamilton, I have a new secret weapon, and I intend to be far more curious going forward!

**Kevin Surace**
**CEO, Appvance**
**Technology Innovator and Speaker**

Great leaders "go beyond what is," in themselves and in the world surrounding them. But before going beyond, each of us must first be courageous and curious enough to do so. *Cracking the Curiosity Code* can help you and your team to "go beyond" and become true innovative leaders of life.

**Kevin Cashman**
**Global Leader of CEO and**
**Executive Development, Korn Ferry Bestselling**
**Author of *Leadership from the Inside Out* and**
***The Pause Principle***

Diane Hamilton has done it—*The Curiosity Code* is like cracking the safe of personal and professional potential.

**Jeffrey Hayzlett, Primetime TV & Podcast**
**Host, Speaker, Author and Part-Time Cowboy**

Dr. Hamilton's excellent exploration of curiosity as a quantifiable success metric will become a benchmark for future leadership courses and life coaches' playbooks.

**Mike Federle,**
**CEO of Forbes Media**

This book helps you to unlock human potential and excel as a great leader. It is a landmark book on curiosity. It is a must read. I wish I had this book long ago. I strongly recommend reading it!

**Professor M.S. Rao, PhD,**
**Father of "Soft Leadership", Author**

Dr. Diane Hamilton's book, *Cracking the Curiosity Code*, made me value the virtue of curiosity even more. To think that curiosity leads one onto a path of greater success has inspired me even more to view life with utmost curiosity, especially when I encounter moments of fear or doubt. It's a fantastically thought-enriching book with steps to help anyone through.

**Sister Jenna,**
**Director, Brahma Kumaris Meditation**
**Museums & Host,**
**America Meditating Radio Show**

# Contents

## Part II: Roadblocks

## Part III: Doing Something about It

# *Foreword*

FROM MY EARLIEST childhood, I can remember both of my parents encouraging my sisters and me to explore. Whether it was my mom, whose motto was "The most important things in life aren't written in a book," or my dad, who had equipped himself with an entire machine shop to tinker and experiment (and work) in. All of us were always asking "Why?" and "Why not?" and "How?"

I was especially intrigued by my dad, whose amazing leadership skills were as great—or greater—than his manufacturing abilities. I was just as curious to learn how he worked with people as I was to learn how he worked with metal.

That curiosity stuck with me, through my education at Purdue University and Harvard, and into my career, from GM to Rasna, to Ariba and DocuSign. Upon reflection, it has served as the key ingredient for being an effective mentor, trusted friend, caring father, and loving husband. What started as an industrial engineer's interest in finding ways to optimize everything broadened into a desire to challenge my own limits—to jump into water over my head—to push myself to keep learning, exploring, and growing.

Along the way, I concluded that, next to integrity and trust, my curiosity and willingness to encourage my colleagues to challenge the status quo was one of the most critical characteristics that propelled us to whatever success we were fortunate enough to experience.

I am a big believer that curiosity is fundamental to transformational leadership and transforming oneself. I also believe that mentor relationships are vital to personal growth, and I've always found that the higher the curiosity on the part of the mentor and the mentee, the richer, more challenging and rewarding the experience.

One of my objectives in business has always been building cultures of curiosity. Bringing diverse teams together, with different temperaments, talents, and convictions, in a culture where it's safe to ask questions and explore, and where there's no such thing as a bad idea, is the catalyst for genius and the secret sauce for transformational change. This kind of open, honest, non-self-righteous culture can create a learning machine that enables organizations to innovate, adapt, scale, and thrive.

In between my various business enterprises, I've had the luxury of taking some time off to be with my children during their formative years. I wanted to expose them to similar, even more challenging experiences, than my parents did for me...from climbing the peak of Mt. Kilimanjaro to exploring the Amazon jungle. I eventually realized that I was employing some of the same tactics with my children that my parents used when I was a child . . . exposing them to experiences and adventures to develop trust, character, and curiosity.

Those characteristics became the cornerstones for me and my career. I assumed trust and character required developing, but believed curiosity was more of an innate characteristic in all of us. Throughout my journey in life, I discovered that curiosity has contagious and catalytic properties. Curiosity spreads like wildfire in an organization and, as I have found out from my five children, the same goes for a family. I have also learned that curiosity is the catalyst for passion, enthusiasm, love, and transformational leadership. In the final analysis, curiosity represents the fundamental basis of my drive.

Dr. Diane Hamilton's book, *Cracking the Curiosity Code*, makes the important point that while we are all born with curiosity, if we allow, it can slip onto the back burner. Somewhere along the way, our curiosity can drift into the background, reducing motivation, engagement, and productivity.

Knowing how vital curiosity has been for my career

and how important it is for companies to have curious workers and leaders, I was intrigued to learn what causes this decline and what we can do to keep curiosity alive and burning.

Before reading Dr. Hamilton's book, I imagined that behavioral scientists had a solid understanding of this topic. We've learned the impact that curiosity has on our everyday lives, especially in the corporate environment. We've learned that there is an almost direct correlation between a company's ability to create new products and services and the curiosity of its workers. And we've learned the price companies pay when the curiosity of their workforce falters.

But the practical questions of why curiosity falters and how we get it back haven't been as well understood as you would expect.

Dr. Diane Hamilton brings insight to each of these issues and more. We learn that curiosity is the catalyst for a variety of other skills and attributes critical to your success, as well as that of your workforce and your company. Attributes such as:

- Decision making
- Conflict resolution
- Employee engagement
- Innovation
- Productivity
- Strategic selling

- Problem solving
- Strategic thinking

Throughout this book, along with the companion assessment instrument and workshop, Diane provides us with the tools needed to examine our levels of engagement with these essential characteristics. And she does it by focusing on that single trait that has been with us since birth, our curiosity.

I hope you enjoy this delightful, yet insightful and informative read. You and your company will be better for it.

Keith Krach

*Keith Krach is a Silicon Valley veteran, best known for being a builder of innovative high-performance companies, a disruptor of paper, and a creator of categories. Krach has led the creation of the categories of Business-to-Business (B2B) Electronic Commerce, Mechanical Design Synthesis, Digital Transaction Management (DTM), and e-Signature and is known as an early pioneer in the robotics industry.*

*As Chairman, CEO & President of DocuSign, Krach spearheaded its transformation from a startup to the category leader and global powerhouse it is today. Under his leadership, DocuSign became a verb, went public, and was awarded Glassdoor's Best Places to Work.*

*Krach co-founded Ariba and, as Chairman & CEO, took the company public, ultimately achieving a market capitalization of $40 billion. In recognition of creating the category of B2B e-Commerce, Ernst & Young named Krach the 2000 National Entrepreneur of the Year and the World Economic Forum honored him with the Technology Pioneer Award.*

*Krach has served as Chairman of the Board of Trustees for Purdue University, Chairman of Angie's List, International President of Sigma Chi Fraternity and was the youngest Vice President in General Motors' history. Krach's alma mater, Purdue University, has honored him with an Honorary Doctorate in Engineering, and the Harvard Business School Alumni Association has named him Business Leader of the Year. Keith is dedicated to paying it forward by mentoring a new generation of transformational leaders in the public, private, and social sectors.*

# PART I

## *It's All Around Us*

# *Prologue*

WE ALL ARE born with a built-in spotlight that's extremely powerful and extraordinarily agile. We can shine it in any direction. We can point it toward things we don't know and things we want to know more about. We can broaden the lens on our spotlight to be expansive, or we can narrow the lens to focus only on a particular subject or set of subjects.

Both animals and babies have spotlights, but infants and toddlers have the lens of their spotlights opened extremely wide. Their focus is all-consuming. They want to know about everything.

That dynamic can continue into adolescence and beyond. Some adults choose to maintain the wide-angle focus they had as children. Others choose not to. As we grow up, we tend to sharpen our focus. When that occurs, our lens becomes narrower and more directed. We seem to be more selective as to where we shine our spotlight.

We can also choose to turn down our spotlights or turn them off altogether, or we can allow external factors to impede their glow. Factors such as fear, assumptions, technology, and social environments can shape their radiance.

Sometimes, for physical or mental reasons, our spotlights can dim. Many believe that to be a natural phenomenon due to aging, but studies show it's more to do with a lack of use than a function of getting old. Fortunately, studies also show that our spotlights can be re-ignited, no matter what our age.

Sometimes, our spotlights can run amok. With ferocious power, at times our spotlight can feel as if it, not us, is in charge. We can be drawn into topics in which we thought we had no interest but find ourselves devoting hours, months, or even years of study to instead.

There is another side to this light-producing phenomenon—darkness.

That's the area in which our spotlights fail to shine, the space where we choose not to know, not to learn, and not to explore. Typically, that choice is due to fear, complacency, technology, arrogance, or pressure from others. Use is what distinguishes the informed from the uninformed, the wise from the unwise, and the successful from the unsuccessful.

Amazing things, our spotlights. They are our means of gaining wisdom, exploring the unknown, escaping ignorance, learning, and growing; they are the means of our very survival.

Is your spotlight turned on?

> The first step towards getting somewhere is to decide you're not going to stay where you are.
>
> *John Pierpont "J.P." Morgan*

# *Introduction*

. . . . . . . . . . . . . . . . . . . . . . . . . . . . . . . . . . . . . . .

The important thing is not to stop questioning.
Curiosity has its own reason for existence. One
cannot help but be in awe when he contemplates
the mysteries of eternity, of life, of the marvelous
structure of reality. It is enough if one tries
merely to comprehend a little of this mystery
each day.

*Albert Einstein*

. . . . . . . . . . . . . . . . . . . . . . . . . . . . . . . . . . . . . . .

T HE SPOTLIGHT DESCRIBED in the Prologue refers to the phenomenon of curiosity or the lack of it. Having taught more than a thousand business courses, I have repeatedly seen this to be true with thousands of students. The success of those who lack curiosity pales in comparison to those who embrace it.

Over the past decade, I have researched the importance of curiosity in improving performance. Through interviewing hundreds of guests on my talk radio show, I have also learned how successful individuals value and develop curiosity.

This phenomenon called curiosity is at the heart of our motivation and our success, no matter our pursuits, whether it's a better job or a more fulfilling life. But there are forces that get in the way. What are those forces? And can they be overcome?

I had to know, and these questions led to this book, *Cracking the Curiosity Code.*

Curiosity is a strong desire to know something. It is defined by scientists in two categories: state and trait curiosity. For example, you could have a fleeting interest and say, "That's an interesting shade of blue. I wonder what it's called." That would be state curiosity.

You could have a reoccurring interest associated with

some type of reward and say, for example, "I've always been interested in having a leadership position, so I need to learn a lot more about financial management." That would be considered trait curiosity.

Understanding the distinction between the two types of curiosity was my first step toward learning how the spotlight within us operates.

*    *    *

Curiosity is not unique to humans. Animals display it, too. The Max Planck Institute coined the term "curiosity gene" based on its work researching a songbird. Their research analyzed the birds' exploratory behavior and found a variation in their level of curiosity, which they were able to pinpoint to a specific gene. That curiosity gene is present in many life forms.

Pursuing whatever makes us curious triggers that gene, and dopamine is released into our bodies when curiosity is triggered. Dopamine is sometimes called the "reward molecule" because it makes us feel good. So, the second thing we learn is that curiosity triggers a satisfying, feel-good sensation that's not dramatically different from eating, drinking, or even enjoying sex.

If curiosity makes us feel good, why don't we try to develop it more? Why don't we sustain that effort throughout our lives?

It's because *things can hold us back from being curious.* Examples of such things are fear, family, societal norms or values, technology that does things for us, and even a sense of "that's the way we've always done it."

Yes, we are constantly in a debate with ourselves about when to be curious and what to be curious about. We must have curiosity to grow and learn. But curiosity, by definition, takes us outside our comfort zone, and that can be scary.

G. Ross Kelly, an author, musician, and songwriter, once told me, "Creativity resides in the unknown and the uncomfortable." So, if we take that leap to explore something new, it's generally because we see a payoff. That's our trait curiosity kicking in.

So I ask:

1. How do we recognize the things that hold us back from exploring our curiosity?

2. How do we maintain and develop our natural sense of curiosity?

3. How do we keep our spotlight bright and ready for deployment?

A friend of mine recently described how she had once been in a funk. After a night of Cabernet-fueled girl talk, she went to bed with wildly conflicting emotions. She concluded that she was stuck in a dead-end job, and by discussing it with her friends, she was spurred to quit moping about it and do something.

She said she had no idea where to begin. She had no

answers but plenty of questions. In the time it took to raise a toast to her friends, she said her curiosity meter had gone from zero to a hundred. Her spotlight had been re-activated.

Just what can make that happen? I mean, besides the wine, of course. How is it that curiosity seems to drift in and out of our lives? How does it go from being dormant one minute to dominating our thoughts the next?

This leads me to ask: why is curiosity such a powerful force? What is the switch mechanism that turns it on and off? This topic intrigues not only behavioral scientists but also employees, leaders, and entrepreneurs who seek to better themselves and want to motivate and encourage others.

I had to know. Yes, I was curious.

\* \* \*

From the earliest days of our efforts to better understand the nuances of human behavior, the subject of curiosity has fascinated behavioral scientists and lay people alike, seemingly more than any other. As early as in ancient Greece, curiosity was seen as an innate force that resides in all of us. In fact, asserting their bold and courageous stance on the topic, a behaviorist once proclaimed that there is some evidence that women possess even more traits of curiosity than men.[1]

Notwithstanding that particularly arcane view on the matter, I have been a highly curious person and assumed others to be the same. But in my lectures and interviews, I discovered deep, vast differences between the curious and the un-curious or the more curious and less curious. I wondered exactly what determines those differences. How did my friend's curiosity seemingly go from zero to one hundred overnight?

My curiosity took me down a long and winding road. I traveled into the minds of highly successful business leaders, innovative entrepreneurs, and, of most interest, the intricate findings of the scientific community who make a living studying topics such as curiosity.

The research from scientists and behaviorists, combined with thoughts and anecdotes from business professionals and entrepreneurs and my own study and those of hundreds of interviewees, make up the sources of this book. It's that compilation of research, analysis, and opinion that I've attempted to sort through and summarize throughout this book. In a simplified, comprehensible fashion, I now present answers to you about what inhibits our curiosity and how we can get it back.

That is my quest.

There are two things you can't find on the internet: answers to questions that have yet to be asked and new ideas. The internet can only tell us what we already know.

*    *    *

As most exploratory ventures begin, my adventure started with a look back in history.

A pioneer of curiosity research was Dr. Daniel Berlyne, a psychologist, philosopher, and professor of psychology who studied at the University of Toronto during the 1960s. His work in the field of experimental and exploratory psychology has served as the foundational research for many scientists who followed.

Berlyne has come to be known as a renowned expert on curiosity and stated that curiosity, or exploratory behavior, is first found to be innate to our very beings, no different from our quests for food and water. He also concluded that curiosity is primarily instigated by three sources:

1.  Novelty: That which is new or unknown to us

2.  Ambiguity: That which is confusing to us

3.  Complexity: That which is known only partially, and we yearn to know more

His research notes the three major drivers of that curiosity:

1.  Uncertainty Reduction: A child picks up an iPad to discover its properties.

2.  Incorporation: The child determines that the iPad lights up when a certain button is pressed.

3. Play or Higher Incorporation: The child learns that they can play games with the iPad.

I could be accused of minimizing or oversimplifying the findings in Berlyne's and others' scientific studies. I hope to do just that. Here's why.

Throughout this journey, my goal will be to provide you with meaningful, science-based information regarding the subject of curiosity, but I'll spare you (as much as possible) its complex analysis and explanations. I offer you digestible, bite-sized chunks of useful information that will help fuel and guide your curiosity. That effort is both for you and for those who look to you for guidance and leadership.

We have learned much about curiosity since those early days of behavioral science. We've discovered why it's essential to how we behave, both in the workplace and as human beings. We continue to learn more about how curiosity drives us and about the critical links between curiosity and intelligence, curiosity and motivation, curiosity and leadership, and the curiosity of well-rounded human beings.

However, the more we study this natural phenomenon, the more it seems we realize how much there is to learn. The sheer complexity of the issue and its endless scientific studies have yielded as much mystery as they have enlightenment. This paradox can be attributed either to the overwhelming volume of examinations of the topic, to our failure to adequately interpret those studies, or both. The net result is an increased appreciation of the value of curiosity in our existence. It leaves a continuing hunger to know more about how we can better apply developing curiosity to our own lives.

Adding complexity to the matter are decades of behavioral data from the workplace to complement the scientific data.

Conclusions come from behavioral scientists, entrepreneurs, and business leaders regarding aspects of curiosity and motivation, curiosity and leadership, and much more.

It brings up more questions: How do the scientific studies correlate to the experiences and performance of business leaders? How do we wade through the myriad of analyses to better understand what we want to know about the subject? How does this analysis affect our ability to lead, have more success, and be better human beings?

If curiosity in all its forms is the cornerstone of innovation and business success, then what form of curiosity drives successful people such as Mark Cuban, Elon Musk, Sheryl Sandberg, Bill Gates, and Warren Buffett? Do they possess some magical dose of curiosity or some other unique characteristic? What drives them to such elevated heights?

If we measure their success strictly in monetary terms, is their curiosity about how they can accumulate more wealth? How surprising would it be to discover that each of them attributes their success, not to money, but to curiosity itself? Then, if we accept the premise that it was their curiosity that drove their success and that curiosity is a trait we all share, what type of curiosity do they possess that sets them apart from the rest of us?

That's the next finding on this journey of discovery: curiosity resides on a spectrum.

*     *     *

Some people ask, "I wonder how butterflies migrate thousands of miles on such delicate wings?" and then they soon forget that inquiry. Others ask, "Is it possible to build an aircraft engineered on the principles of a butterfly's wings?" and then they turn that thought into action. Most of us fall somewhere in the middle.

When the internet was in its infancy, we likely pondered its endless possibilities. Many entrepreneurs dabbled in the potential of this new frontier, while others achieved success from the emerging technology. With it came many whose curiosity and courage catapulted them to unprecedented heights.

Mark Cuban, for example, called his curiosity the "underlying fire" that caused him to create a successful business by having radio frequencies transmitted over the newly created worldwide web. As a result, he changed the face of the commercial radio business and became a multi-billionaire. What transformed his curiosity into a passion and motivation, yet left others only mildly curious?

How does curiosity become motivation? Can it be learned? Can the rest of us turn our casual curiosity into a passionate curiosity to fuel our drive to succeed, to become a highly successful leader, and to achieve whatever goals that, today, we may only dream about?

What if?

*    *    *

As I said, I'm highly curious. While I wouldn't put myself in the league of Mark Cuban or Steve Forbes, people tell me that my curiosity level is on their side of the spectrum. My own curiosity most likely comes from two factors.

First, I was born of parents who never worked in traditional jobs, so I didn't have role models to emulate how a driven, type A personality should behave. That void made me more curious.

When I was a kid, I had to figure out things on my own. Often feeling bored, I would use my creativity. I made clothes for my Barbie dolls. I created my own Diane's Diner with three items on the menu I learned to prepare. I served lunch to my parents and anyone else I could coax into eating one of my three entrees.

I knew I had a mind for business. When I was young,

I was interested in checkbooks, typewriters, and cash registers. That was a big signal. For Diane's Diner, I liked the idea of having menus, items to sell, customer service, and all the things I later learned were business related. I had to resort to my own devices to avoid boredom, so I took advantage of my curiosity.

Then, in my national Take the Lead radio talk show (http://drdianehamiltonradio.com/), I interviewed hundreds of entrepreneurs and successful leaders of all types. I heard the stories of Steve Forbes (Editor-in-Chief of *Forbes*), Craig Newmark (Founder of Craigslist), Keith Krach (Chairman of DocuSign), Roya Mahboob (*Time* magazine's Most Influential People in the World), and many others.

My interviews made me curious to know what drove my guests' success.

Once they achieved what's considered more than enough wealth, what continued to drive them? Was it the desire for more wealth?

Well, they each told me the same thing: acquiring wealth was a bi-product of their inner motivation.

So, what is it? Ego? A desire to make the world a better place? A fundamental desire to help people? What continues to drive their relentless pursuits? One word keeps coming up from each of them; you guessed it, *curiosity*.

Each of them has shared highly diverse stories from a variety of different circumstances. But given all their

differences, curiosity seemed to be the common thread
for each of them.

> I think, at a child's birth, if a mother could ask a
> fairy godmother to endow it with the most useful
> gift, that gift would be curiosity.
>
> *Eleanor Roosevelt*

Now, I assume most people desire money and wealth.
But from listening to successful business leaders, it
seems that curiosity, not the pursuit of wealth, is by far
the more powerful motivator of the two. The money is a
mere by-product.

And the studies—oh, the studies! There is more
scientific data about curiosity than we'll ever understand,
much less apply in our own lives. It's made me wonder,
where is there a simple sourcebook from which to
extract all the things that scientists have learned and
apply them to become better employees, better leaders,
or better human beings?

If there is, I have not found it, and I have searched
intensely. Still, the questions abound. Go to Wikipedia
to learn what provokes our curiosity and, based on
hits to its webpages, you'll see everything from Kim
Kardashian to Michael Jackson to Tupac Shakur to
Donald Trump. Google's list of searches ranges from

how to play Pokémon Go, to how to make slime, to how to play Powerball.

Yet human curiosity goes deeper than those topics. According to the five-factor model of personality, for example, openness to new experiences is one of the main components of our personality.

Further, we are told that survival, the pursuit of novelty, and the need to fill our information gaps are at the root of our curiosity.

This is in line with the questions I wish to pursue. Specifically,

- Where do I fit on the curiosity spectrum between mildly and extremely curious?

- Can increased curiosity make me a more successful leader?

- Does my fear of failure impede my curiosity?

- Does my curiosity diminish as I age?

- Can I learn to better cultivate my curiosity?

- Does curiosity translate into motivation or success?

These types of questions have befuddled me greatly, both from my studies as a specialist on human behavior and from my many interviews of strong business leaders. These types of questions have led me into the briar patch of numerous scientific studies on the subject and prompted me to write this book.

Through all my research, I have yet to find a concise, comprehensive, and practical means of knowing how we can harness the curiosity that lingers within each of us and to convey that information with clarity. Both for my benefit as a professional and the benefit of my listeners and readers, my goals are twofold:

1. to decipher and simplify the myriad of studies and analyses on the topic, and

2. to provide a clear and concise way to both understand and apply the topic so that people can become

   - More engaged and productive at work,
   - More effective leaders who foster a positive work culture that supports improved productivity and engagement, and
   - Better-rounded individuals.

Ultimately, I ask you to determine how successful I have been in accomplishing these objectives once you're read this book. At a minimum, I hope that I spark your curiosity, and I certainly hope that you enjoy the ride.

# Chapter 1

# Survival:
# The Mother of All Curiosity

Necessity is the mother of invention.

*Anonymous*

CURIOSITY, PART OF our DNA, is no different from our pursuit of food, water, or sex. Our bodies are programmed to be curious and reward us when we exercise that curiosity. It is our body's way of encouraging us to find new sources of food, new means of protecting ourselves, and new ways to aid us in times of crisis.

This deep, intrinsic force guides a curiosity that has caused scientists to refer to us as "informavores," constantly seeking and digesting information. Even when our curiosity guides us on pursuits that appear to be a waste of time, our body finds a way to remind us that what we might not find useful today could be extremely useful tomorrow.

Like other animals, humans are learning machines.

Psychologist Jean Piaget says that we come into this world as tiny amateur scientists. From the first time we discover our own hands, we embark on a nonstop experiment to discover everything. This natural phenomenon aids in our survival in the searching of food and fending off threats.

This perpetual search not only helps us survive but also serves as the beginnings of our emotional intelligence. By teaching us to form bonds with others and develop empathy, we learn to incorporate others into our survival efforts.

The founder of modern psychology, William James, explained that curiosity is an impulse toward better cognition, one that leads us to how we acquire knowledge through experience. When we are curious, our brain anticipates a reward, dopamine is released, and we gain a sense of well-being. Just as we gain a sense of reward from eating, sex, or winning the lottery, we get a rush from learning something new.

Endless subsequent studies have linked curiosity to our survival as a species. Neuroscientists Ethan Bromberg-Martin and Okihie Hikosaka were the first to discover this curiosity-dopamine reaction in their extensive research with monkeys.[2]

Professor Evan Polman from the University of Wisconsin demonstrated that our curiosity levels change as we encounter different situations.[3] Additionally, in a series of studies, Drs. Oliver Robins, James Demetre, and Jordan Litman demonstrated that, when confronted with a crisis, people are apt to be more curious.[4] In fact, curiosity aids them in their efforts to cope with crises.

In stress and at other times, our curiosity can drive us to the extreme. In *For the Time Being*,[5] Annie Dillard tells the story of British officer James Taylor, who in the 1930s was stationed in what is now Papua, New Guinea. With the aid of his military aircraft, Taylor made contact with people in a mountain village perched 3,000+ feet above sea level.

The villagers had never seen a trace of the outside world, much less an airplane. After spending time with the local tribe and completing his studies, Taylor made plans to depart. As he prepared to leave, one of the villagers, using vines cut from the jungle, tied himself to the fuselage of Taylor's airplane shortly before it took off. The villager explained calmly to his loved ones that, no matter what happened to him, he had to see where this strange craft came from.

According to Rabbi David Wolpe of Sinai Temple in Los Angeles, that astonishing act of courage arises from a deep human need within all of us to understand, discover, explore, and follow the thread back to the beginning. "Living in the world is not enough," he proclaimed. "We share a hunger to decipher its mysteries."[6]

That deep-seated curiosity can lead to both survival and self-sacrifice. Maurice Samuel, writer, historian, and chronicler of Judaism, stated that curiosity is the secret of the basic survival of the Jewish people. Early on, he explained, the Jews decided that they were not going to disappear until they figured out how things worked. Strapped to the metaphorical fuselage, we are still here, Samuel said, seeking to understand.[7]

Why did humankind travel to the moon? Why are our sights set on Mars? We humans are deeply curious beings, and the more urgent the need to sustain our very survival, the more powerful our curiosity about the surroundings we occupy.

According to a study performed at Harvard University, Hemmelder and Blanchard concluded that our economy, our society, and our very existence are strongly shaped by our drive to obtain information. They called humans "informavores," creatures who search for and digest information just as carnivores hunt for and eat meat. Described from an evolutionary perspective, "There is a clear reason why we, like all animals, seek out information: it is vital to our survival and reproduction. A bird that spent its whole life eating berries from a single bush and never explored its environment could be missing out on a much better food source nearby. Thus, it is not surprising that exploration, hence curiosity, is common, if not universal in the animal world."[8]

These researchers further explained that monkeys, for example, will push a button at high rates of speed just for an opportunity to peek out of a window. They found that roundworms do not crawl to a food source directly. Rather, they circle toward it in a way that gives them the most information about their environment.

The researchers also described curiosity-driven behaviors in very young animals, even before they've had enough experience to learn the association between knowledge and rewards. For example, human newborns tend to stare at new visual scenes for a much longer time than they look at known visual scenes.[9]

Animals tend to learn over the course of their lives that a greater knowledge of their environment leads to greater rewards, such as food or other essential resources. They are continuously in survival mode, asking, "Where's my next meal coming from? How do I protect myself from predators? Where will I sleep tonight?" As a result, they are constantly curious. Even domesticated animals never lose that intrinsic curiosity. They may have it cushy today, but they never know if and when it will all end. Even pets that get all the creature comforts a human can provide are constantly on alert.

By contrast, there are humans who conclude that they have advanced beyond survival mode and have lost that intrinsic instinct. If they have less uncertainty, they have less curiosity.

But that's certainly not true of humans who have some form of malady. Like animals, theirs can be a life of continuous survival, and as a result, endless curiosity.

Consider Erik Weihenmayer, author of *Touch the Top of the World, The Adversity Advantage,* and *No Barriers.*[10] Besides being an author, filmmaker, and speaker, Erik is first and foremost an adventurer.

Erik is also blind, which means living a life in survival mode and being constantly curious. For Erik, it has also meant being constantly daring. Despite going blind at age fourteen, he pursued his life of adventure. On May 25, 2001, he became the only blind person to reach the summit of Mount Everest. At age thirty-nine, he reached the top of Carstensz Pyramid, completing his quest to climb all seven summits, the highest peaks on each of the seven continents. *Time* magazine wrote: "There's no way to put what Erik has done into perspective because no one's ever done anything like it."[11]

Erik's greatest achievements are by-products of his enormous curiosity. He had no choice but to be curious; he had to survive without sight in a seeing world.

*   *   *

Other studies have suggested that survival is at the root of the pursuit of information itself because it's intrinsically rewarding. The reason primary rewards such as food and sex are pleasurable is that animals that enjoy eating and reproducing are more likely to survive and produce offspring. Evolution has therefore developed an internal reward system to drive behaviors that help animals acquire the resources they need. Could this same reward system be prompting information-seeking behavior in humans?

Learning seems intrinsically rewarding.

Let's review. Curiosity, intrinsic and fundamental to our very being, is referred to as trait curiosity. In contrast, state curiosity is the type of curiosity driven by external factors such as money, prestige, and power. Trait curiosity affirms that humans are hard-wired to have a lifelong interest in learning and to explore what's new to them.

Scientists caution us, however, that our trait curiosity can drive both good and bad behaviors, from arson to drug experimentation to fearlessness of all kinds. But curiosity is viewed overall as a positive characteristic.

Scientists also tell us that, while trait curiosity is an inherent characteristic, it can be more prominent in some people than in others. That begs the question of how we know when someone exhibits a high degree of trait curiosity, a strong intrinsic desire to learn and grow. It also prompts us to ask, is that intrinsic curiosity constantly active? Or must it be aroused? Or must we rely more heavily on external measures, our state curiosity, which includes money or prestige?

*   *   *

I have been told I was curious since my earliest days as a child. Can that curiosity be attributed to my trait curiosity inherent in my nature? Or was it my surroundings or circumstances? Whatever it was, it seemed to require no external drive or motivation. In effect, I relied on my own ingenuity to survive, and I believed it was due to my curiosity as much as anything else.

As I said, neither of my parents held traditional jobs. One was legally blind, and the other was largely a caretaker. They had little guidance to offer in the ways of the work world or a traditional lifestyle. At an early age, I found myself gravitating to other family members for such guidance.

As I reflect on those years now, my curiosity seemed instinctual, the core of my survival. The strength of my curiosity became apparent to me in my youth, and I've been working on developing curiosity ever since.

One of my radio guests was Steve Forbes, chairman and editor-in-chief of *Forbes* magazine and a former U.S. presidential candidate. He credited his roots in conservatism to curiosity: "I, like everyone else, had a yearning to know why things happen. Why do disasters happen? Where things go right, where things go wrong—you continuously learn about it and get a greater understanding of how to endure, survive, and move forward."

Ken Fisher, a world-famous investment guru, described in an interview with me how curiosity and survival form the core of his keys to sound investments: "Most investors fail not because of a lack of training or knowledge, but because humans are hard-wired, through millennia of evolution, to deal with survival problems. We are not hard-wired to deal with capital markets, which are inherently counterintuitive.

"But you can counteract that. You can learn how your brain deceives you and retrain it to see markets properly. Once you do that, you will no longer be fooled by conventional investment advice or blind to remarkable patterns. *You will know what others don't.*"[12]

Wherever we turn and whatever we choose to pursue in our lives, the forces that drive us can be traced to that innate curiosity we actively use as infants. Our same curiosity to learn our surroundings and survive can guide us today.

But many questions remain about this powerful force embedded in each of us and how it serves as an essential tool for our survival. For example, why are some types of information more tantalizing to us than others? Why are we all so different from each other and interested in different things?

It's curiosity that urges me to dig deeper into this intriguing phenomenon.

*Chapter 2*

# Curiosity, Motivation, and Drive

. . . . . . . . . . . . . . . . . . . . . . . . . . . . . . . . . . . . . . . . .

No one asks how to motivate a baby. A baby
naturally explores everything it can get at, unless
restraining forces have already been at work.
And this tendency doesn't die out; it's wiped out.

*B.F. Skinner*

. . . . . . . . . . . . . . . . . . . . . . . . . . . . . . . . . . . . . . . . .

WHAT MOTIVATES US? And what is the correlation, if any, between motivation and curiosity?

Assuming the two are connected, which happens first? Does motivation drive us to curiosity? Or does curiosity lead to motivation?

These are the types of questions I had to find answers to.

Again, I was curious.

For example, did my curiosity about the subject of curiosity motivate me to write this book? Or was I already motivated, and therefore became curious to learn more about the subject so I could write it? Let's go back to the beginning.

Curiosity is described by behavioral scientists as a quality related to inquisitive thinking such as exploration, investigation, and learning, as is evident from observation of humans and other animals. Motivation is described by those same behavioral scientists as the reason for people's actions, desires, and needs.[13]

Motivation is why we do what we do. We can typically find motivation for taking a certain action or believing a certain way by filling in the blank: I do an action because _____. I exercise because I want to be healthy when I am older. I work at my current job because I need the benefits. A motive is what prompts us to act in a certain way, or at least to develop an inclination for a specific behavior.

Okay, so curiosity is the interest to learn more about a subject; motivation is the desire to do something with that information.

From my own studies, from the scientific research, and from the stories of professionals and motivational speakers interviewed on my program, there's agreement that our motivation is driven by a combination of three factors:

1. Need: We need to sustain ourselves. We need to provide for ourselves and our families, and we need to have a place to live. Therefore, we are motivated.

2. Desire or want: We desire a certain type of house or car or a membership at the country club. We do not need these things, but we want them, so we are motivated.

3. Some missing element or void: We suffer some forms of shortcoming in our lives, whether mental, physical, or emotional. To varying degrees, we have a desire to overcome or attempt to mitigate those shortcomings. It's that desire that motivates us.

We've heard about individuals who overcame trying situations to accomplish great things. Consider the story of Leonard Kim. His motivation was driven by a different need, the need to survive.

This successful entrepreneur went from being homeless to becoming the managing partner at InfluenceTree, a personal branding consulting firm that has amassed a social media following of well over 500,000 people.

Leonard's motivation drove him to become a leading expert whose content has been read more than ten million times. That need led to his curiosity and ultimately to the counter-intuitive proposition in his TEDx talk he called "Why You Should Let Your Fears Guide You."[14]

Rather than trying to escape your fears, this entrepreneur advised, run toward them and embrace them to find your motivation and purpose.

> It took me losing everything to realize the true importance of curiosity. I had to reset my mind, body, and soul and start fresh.
>
> *Leonard Kim*

Others are motivated by the notion that something is missing in their lives. The most vivid examples can be found in individuals who have physical drawbacks. From blind musicians such as Ray Charles and Stevie

Wonder to the extraordinary achievements of Helen Keller, there are millions of people whose motivation and curiosity have been enhanced by a void in their sensory abilities.

Another guest, Robin Farmanfarmaian, was misdiagnosed with an autoimmune disease as a teenager. It resulted in countless hospitalizations and surgeries, not to mention the virtual loss of normalcy in her teen years. Her experience motivated her to become an expert in health care. This author, speaker, and serial entrepreneur was driven by the belief that technology can empower patients and create a positive impact in the health and medical fields.[15]

Another guest, Lance Collin Allred, grew to become a gangly near- seven-footer who was deaf. His deafness combined with his height motivated him to become the first legally deaf professional basketball player in the history of the National Basketball Association (NBA). He later became a recognized inspirational speaker, author, and TEDx presenter with his talk "What Is Your Polygamy?"[16]

Tanner Gers embarked on a similar path but for a very different reason. Tanner lost his sight at age twenty-one after losing control of his car in an auto accident. Since that day, despite being blind, Tanner graduated from college and became a 2011 Para Pan American gold medalist, 2012 U.S. Paralympic trials gold medalist, 2012 Paralympian, 2013 World Championship team member, two-time National Beep Baseball Association World Series Offensive MVP, and four-time Offensive All-Star. He is also a published author and motivational speaker.

These individuals are like many who have suffered similar mishaps or shortcomings, be they mental, emotional, or physical. Driven by those shortcomings, they illustrate the power of curiosity and motivation.

*   *   *

> Human beings have an innate inner drive to be autonomous, self-determined, and connected to one another. And when that drive is liberated, people achieve more and live richer lives.
>
> *Daniel H. Pink*

To uncover some misconceptions about what drives us, I found insights in the book, *Drive: The Surprising Truth About What Motivates Us*, by Daniel H. Pink.[17]

In his book, Pink provided an interesting study of how reward, fear, and punishment play into our drive, motivation, and curiosity. Fear and punishment, he concluded, do not motivate us or give us the drive to want to be more curious. Rather, our desire to learn and explore is better driven by reward and by viewing learning as a choice rather than a requirement.

Pink highlighted three elements that drive our motivation: a need for autonomy, a need for mastery, and a need for purpose. He explained how intrinsic motivations are renewable, like solar power and pointed out that those who are intrinsically motivated will outperform those driven by external rewards. Therefore, it's important to focus on the internal rewards that we can realize from developing a sense of curiosity.

Pink also described how our early childhood can play into our curiosity and drive. If we're involved in actions and behaviors that we don't find rewarding, we won't continue to explore new ones. If people lack curiosity toward something, they might have received a negative consequence for pursuing things in the past. For example, if parents used negative reinforcement to get their kids to avoid exploration, the child might fear exploring.

While curiosity might spur the release of dopamine, if we have had enough negative rewards associated with exploration, it could have a much different impact. That's what causes us to recall past incidents and how we were rewarded or punished for inquisitive behaviors.

Further, not all things will be equally fascinating to us upon discovery. If we explore an area that we find uninteresting, it's important not to give up and assume that exploration is a waste of time. Rather, it indicates that perhaps other areas of exploration might be more rewarding.

*   *   *

There are endless studies on the interconnections between curiosity and motivation. There is also ample research on how much of our curiosity is intrinsic, or internally driven, and how much is externally driven. (We will examine this further in subsequent chapters.)

Regarding this linkage between motivation and curiosity, we ask: can you have one without the other? Is it possible to be curious but not motivated?

Conversely, we ask: is it possible to be motivated but not curious about what motivates us? How does that work?

The answer appears to be "yes" to the first questions and "yes but probably ill-advised" to the second pair.

At one time or another, each of us has been determined to improve our health and fitness, for example. We were curious enough to explore various ways of achieving that goal. We researched diet and exercise recommendations. We explored gym memberships. We studied different types of exercise machines for the home. Some of us even purchased the exercise equipment and set it up, then we only used it as a clothes rack. Thus, we were curious enough to explore the possibilities, but not quite motivated enough to act. Yes, we were curious but not motivated.

In other circumstances, we decided to begin an exercise regimen, such as jogging. We eagerly embarked on our first five-mile run without researching how to best do it. We probably ended up out of breath after the first 500 yards, unable to bend over to tie our shoes the next day, and determined never to jog again. We were motivated but not curious enough to explore the subject well, and we paid the price.

Going deeper into the scientific realm, in his classic 1890 publication *The Principles of Psychology*,[18] William James described two other types of curiosity.

The first is an instinctual arousal to an unfamiliar object. Imagine our fascination being introduced to our first computer. That fascination, according to the famed psychiatrist, was instinctual. The second type of curiosity is what James described as a scientific curiosity and metaphysical wonder in which the "brain responds to an inconsistency or a gap in its knowledge, just as the musical brain responds to a discord in what it hears."[19]

The underlying belief was that either form of curiosity was sufficient to compel us to some form of motivation. Hence, curiosity yielded motivation.

For the longest time, that belief seemed to withstand scientific scrutiny. In the early twentieth century, scientists assumed that curiosity was one of the basic human drives, along with hunger, thirst, and sex. But the research took a new twist when researcher Daniel Berlyne found more nuance to the connection between curiosity and motivation.

Berlyne also divided curiosity into two types, which

he described as diversive curiosity and specific curiosity. Diversive curiosity is akin to casual or fleeting curiosity, a general tendency for a person to seek novelty, take risks, or search for adventure. Specific curiosity is a more proactive type of curiosity, the desire to investigate a specific object or problem to better understand it.

Berlyne further concluded that curiosity can be aroused by external stimuli such as complexity, novelty, uncertainty, and conflict. And here's the important part: if an external stimulus is too low, there will be no motivation to explore it. If a stimulus is too high, it will result in anxiety, almost paralysis. If it's just right, it will result in the desired exploratory behavior.

For example, think of the end of your company's fiscal year when the bosses want you to meet and exceed your financial quotas. If the incentive is only a five-dollar bonus for another sale, it hardly seems worth the effort. On the other extreme, if the incentive is a $10,000 bonus for fifty more sales, it may seem out of reach and therefore equally non-motivating. According to the research, we are motivated only when the stimulus seems reasonable and attainable.

Hence, motivation is tied to the levels of curiosity with which we are presented. Just like Goldilocks and her three bears, if the curiosity is too low, we're not interested. If it is too high, we're scared off. However, if it's just right, we're motivated to act on it.

Other studies have suggested the same. Our knowledge gaps, which are the basis of our curiosity, must feel manageable for us to be motivated to act on them. Consider the animal that seems curious about your presence and even exhibits a desire to come closer, yet it is repelled by the fear of the unknown, the unmanageable.

Berlyne concluded that curiosity and thus motivation are aroused by a combination of complexity, novelty, uncertainty, and fear. But what about the curiosity and motivation that have no tangible benefit? What is it that motivates video gamers to undertake endless challenges for no traditional reward?

For example, what induced millions of people around the world to play a video game called Cube? The game (originally titled Curiosity but changed to avoid confusion with the Mars explorer of the same name) is a collection of cubes or cubelets to navigate through to get to the center. Indeed, it's a high-tech version of the popular Christmas wrapping game in which a gift is embedded in multiple layers of wrapping paper. Participants or recipients are challenged to get to the final layer of paper and find the gift.

In most video games (excluding Cube), there is no prize other than the social reward of competing with others to win the game. Scientists tell us that the same intrinsic drive that motivates us to be social is the same drive that motivates us to be curious. So, the social interaction is motivation in and of itself.

\*   \*   \*

It is clear that curiosity and motivation are essential to our being productive, healthy, and happy. It is also clear that the two must work hand-in-hand for us to achieve whatever goals we set for ourselves: personal, professional, or altruistic.

Further, our curiosity and motivation can take us in positive and constructive directions or toward less positive or sinister outcomes. That's where choice comes into play.

There have been additional studies asking which comes first, curiosity or motivation, and what differentiates the mildly curious and motivated from the passionately curious and motivated and everyone in between. (These topics will also be tackled in chapters to come.)

For now, we conclude that, like love and marriage, horses and carriages, peanut butter and jelly, curiosity and motivation must go together to function properly, regardless of which came first.

Consider advertising campaigns. They are designed first and foremost to arouse our curiosity. That curiosity is intended to motivate us to explore the product or service and ultimately buy it. These are called teaser campaigns. Mercedes had an appealing ad, where two young men watch a new car on a computer screen that remains hidden from the viewer. Their reactions entice consumers to know more about the product.

Consider the Rubik's cube. Not until we are exposed to its complexity are we curious, and therefore motivated, to find the solution.

Consider the mystery of Malaysian Airlines Flight 370, or the cliffhanging soap operas, or the many crime dramas on television. Our curiosity compels us to follow them.

Consider the tragic saga of Scott Peterson and his pregnant wife, Laci. What kept us glued to our televisions to see the case brought to justice? Curiosity.

So, which is it? Does our curiosity stimulate and provoke our drive and motivation? Or does our motivation and drive spur our curiosity?

Stated another way, are we curious only about the things we are motivated to learn or do? Or are we motivated or driven to pursue initiatives without being curious to learn more about them?

According to behavioral scientists, it depends. However, the consensus is that it's our curiosity that serves as the driving force.

Whether it's in combination with the drivers Berlyne described, uncertainty, novelty, complexity, or conflict, or not, it's ultimately our curiosity that fuels our motivation.

*Chapter 3*

# Curiosity and Decision-Making

. . . . . . . . . . . . . . . . . . . . . . . . . . . . . . . . . . . . .

You're always one decision away from
a completely different life.

*Mel Robbins*

. . . . . . . . . . . . . . . . . . . . . . . . . . . . . . . . . . . . .

Intuitively, we know that curiosity plays a role in our decision-making, but how does that work?

Research presented in 2016 found that curiosity has an impact on decision-making. By piquing people's curiosity, leaders can have the potential to increase desired behaviors, which can be important for people who might otherwise lack motivation.

In a study by Evan Polman,[20] people were given a choice of two fortune cookies, one plain and one dipped in chocolate. Participants whose curiosity was piqued by being told that the plain cookie contained a fortune specifically about them overwhelmingly chose the plain cookie by 71 percent. In contrast, when participants were told nothing, 80 percent chose the chocolate-dipped cookie.

This tells us that people might need to experience closure when their curiosity has been piqued. The fortune cookie experiment demonstrated that "curiosity-based interventions come at an incredibly small cost and could help steer people toward a variety of positive actions."[21]

Curious observation can be considered the first step in the decision-making process. Among the things that curiosity puts into motion are questioning, inquiring about things, experimentation, visualization, skepticism, evaluation, identification of different patterns, imaginative thought, logical reasoning, prediction, inference, etc.

Thus, curiosity leads to observations in which we're able to recognize issues or problems before making decisions. If we feel a sense of dissatisfaction with a situation, through curious observation we can set in motion the process to make decisions that will produce better outcomes.

Perhaps one of the biggest ways that curiosity affects decision-making is that it gives us more choices. By uncovering options, we have a better chance of reaching a more effective solution to the problem at hand.

High performers often must make tough decisions. They maintain their mental acuity in ways such as being voracious readers. In our interview, what stood out for billionaire Naveen Jain was just how much time he spent reading. His curiosity helped him learn about new areas of research or unfamiliar topics. Running a billion-dollar company requires a lot of decision-making. To ensure that he makes good ones, Naveen and leaders like him spend a lot of time reading.

Julian Hayes II in *Inc.* magazine explained it this way: "Exposing yourself to new ideas and environments is powerful because of its effects on your brain chemistry and outlook on the world which leads to healthier *decision-making*. At the basis of all of this lies *curiosity* which is a key driver for innovation along with improving your working memory."[22]

In *Harvard Business Review*, Dr. Terri Cooper, principal and chief inclusion officer at Deloitte Consulting LLP, shared insights from what she learned regarding the six signature traits of inclusive leadership. These six signature traits are cultural intelligence, collaboration, commitment, courage, cognizance, and curiosity. As she explained, "*Curiosity* isn't passive. It's very active. *Curiosity's* about showing appreciative inquiry, bringing open mindset and true desire to know your people. Leaders who show these traits actively seek the perspective of diverse others in ideation and *decision-making*."[23]

It seems that the more curious people are, the more alternatives they're able to generate when making tough decisions. Some may prefer the simplistic approach (e.g., Do I choose A or B, black or white?). However, those who actively engage their curiosity to generate more alternatives always seem to make better, higher quality decisions.

\*   \*   \*

In my work, I'm frequently involved in decisions to select speakers and interviewees for my presentations and radio shows. Since I've been deliberating on this topic of curiosity, I've become increasingly curious about some of my decisions.

Sometimes, I find myself choosing based on biographies alone. Other times, I sense something about a potential guest that makes me want to know more. It could be a photograph, a tagline, or a seemingly insignificant reference in a bio that attracts my attention. I often review several bios that may seem similar, and I end up selecting people based on my gut instinct.

Michelle Tillis Lederman is a perfect example. I chose her to speak at a recent *Forbes* event. Here's why.

Michelle was named one of *Forbes'* Top 25 Networking Experts. A CEO, she has written three books and been featured in the *Wall Street Journal* and *New York Times*. Others I considered had equally as remarkable backgrounds as Michelle. However, in retrospect, I chose her because of gut instinct as much as her impressive résumé. My instinct paid off because she delivered an impactful speech.

This is where experience becomes part of the calculation. Having made hundreds of choices in just as many similar situations, I let my gut decide, and based on my experience, when all else is equal, my gut has served me well.

*    *    *

### *Five Fundamental Steps of Decision-Making*

Decision-making, as classically described, involves these five fundamental steps:

1.  Define the problem or issue.

2.  Define the goal or resolution.

3.  Generate alternative solutions that could achieve the goal.

4.  Analyze and decide which alternative best achieves the goal.

5.  Implement the selected alternative.

Sounds simple, right?

However, these five steps do not always lead to a positive outcome. Some major decisions that employed this formula have led to disastrous results.

For example, dating as far back as the 1950s, Ford Motor Company used this process to decide how best to compete with the ever-popular '57 Chevy. That decision resulted in the Edsel, a car that failed badly in the marketplace.

In the 1980s, Kodak dominated the photography market worldwide. As the age of technology emerged, the company owned the patents to an obscure phenomenon called digital photography. The leaders feared that if they productized and sold the new technology, it would cause a decline in their film sales. Using the classic decision-making process, they decided to forgo the new technology to protect their dominance in film-based photography. Of course, digital photography took over the industry, and if the company had focused more on digitization, chances are it would be thriving today.

In 2000, an obscure video company called Netflix pitched an offer to Blockbuster, the most dominant player in the video rentals market, to become a partner for online rentals. After analyzing the offer using this standard model, Blockbuster's leaders concluded that there was little or no market for online video rentals. They decided to pass on the offer. What happened? Blockbuster went out of business, and in 2018, Netflix had 124 million paying subscribers in over 190 countries and $7.6 billion in revenue.[24]

So much for this decision-making process as a standalone method for making sound decisions.

Both industry and government organizations have been applying this standard decision-making process since the creation of business schools, yet both are littered with disastrous results. So, what *does* lead to sound, creative decision-making? And what role, if any, does curiosity play in our decision-making process? Does it aid or hinder it? Is curiosity even a factor? Should it play a more prominent role?

My research says absolutely yes.

For example, curiosity has been used to increase traffic to websites with enticing headlines such as,

"You won't believe what happened next," or "You'll be shocked when you see this." Called "click bait," these headlines typically aim to exploit our curiosity gap by providing just enough information to make us curious but not enough to satisfy that curiosity without clicking the link. We want to obtain the desired information.

OK, so we know that we can be enticed by our curiosity. But can our curiosity serve as a guide in making better and smarter decisions?

My research again says yes. In fact, scientists say that curiosity is the first step in our decision-making process, though unconsciously so in many cases. Behaviorists use the term "curious observation" to describe this phenomenon.

Researchers have shown that when people are confronted with choices, we are instinctively more curious about some choices than we are about others. They conclude that we should train our curiosity to become more explicit in that process. By making a more conscious effort to apply that to potential choices, we gain more knowledge about each particular option. In that way, we become smarter about selecting or de-selecting those options.

*   *   *

Whether consciously or unconsciously, curious observation is inherent in considering alternatives in the decision-making process. Scientists simply encourage us to be more explicit, more conscious in applying this natural phenomenon as part of our decision-making.

We've heard the phrase "seize the moment." In this case, we're encouraged to seize the curiosity. That curiosity, according to the research, stimulates a variety of other healthy processes including questioning, experimentation, visualization, skepticism, evaluation, identification of different patterns, imaginative thought, logical reasoning, prediction, and inference. Collectively, these curiosity-driven processes are inclined to lead to smarter decisions.

It's through these things combined, curiosity and observation or curious observation, that we make decision-making easier and more effective.

> Don't be intimidated by what you don't know.
> That can be your greatest strength and ensure that
> you do things differently from everyone else.
>
> *Sara Blakely*

\* \* \*

What about the range of alternatives we allow ourselves to consider in making bold or difficult decisions? Do we have the proper mindset to explore creative, out-of-the-box options in our decision-making process?

Stanford psychologist Carol Dweck researched how

our mindset affects our decision-making process, especially when in a competitive or challenging situation requiring new, creative ideas.

In her work, she found that having a fixed mindset (limited ability to be open to new ideas) has a dramatic effect on being able to seek out creative alternatives. When our situation requires us to consider fresh, off-the-wall ideas for solutions, having an open mindset is critical.[25]

As researchers suggest, being open to considering unusual or unheard-of alternatives and vigorously applying curiosity to each of those alternatives are critical. If these two things are happening, we become more effective decision-makers.

In 1968, the USS *Pueblo*, a spy ship, was fired upon and captured by North Korean military forces.[26] One American was killed, and the remaining crew members were held captive. The incident became a major political crisis for President Lyndon Johnson, and the entire country became fervently anti-Korean, North or South.

About this time, Burger King, the fast-food giant, was scheduled to entertain Korean executives at its national headquarters in hopes of expanding into the Asian market. Burger King leaders had planned to fly the flag of their guests in front of their headquarters for the visit. The local community was in an uproar, and news of the pending visit quickly spread across the United States.

Burger King leaders were confronted with two options. One was the unenviable choice of offending their guests and potentially losing the prospects of expanding into the entire emerging Asian market. The other was losing the loyalty and trust of their local community and customers across the country. Either way, it felt like a lose-lose proposition.

"Would Burger King executives be willing to consider a third, more off-the-wall alternative?" one employee asked. "What if a maintenance truck 'accidentally' backed over the flagpole, requiring the flag ceremony to be held indoors, out of the view of the local community?" The executives would profusely apologize for the unusual circumstance to their foreign visitors, he suggested. At the same time, they would protect their reputation and market viability with U.S. customers. And that's what Burger King did.

In this case, openness to creative alternatives and the curiosity to explore them saved the day.

\*   \*   \*

There is, of course, a potential downside in unleashing our curiosity to generate more creative alternatives. We're talking about that dreaded decision-making roadblock, analysis paralysis.

As we become more curious, we obtain more information. As we obtain more information, we consider more choices. When do we stop the process of exploring and simply decide? Can curiosity help us with that?

Once again, researchers say yes.

We are reminded that curiosity is considered an intrinsic motivation, which means that we derive some fundamental reward from exploring alternatives during the decision-making process.

This is where intuition steps in. That is, the same curiosity that helps us to generate creative alternatives also tells us when we've reached a point of diminishing returns and it's time to decide.

Like curious observation and openness to new ideas, intuition is essential in creative decision-making, especially when we lack knowledge about an unfamiliar topic. Intuition, accompanied by curiosity, helps us know when we have enough knowledge, when to close down the exploration, and when to act.

In *What Makes an Effective Executive,* Peter Drucker, the famous management guru, says, "Before you can make the right decision, get the knowledge you need."[27]

Curiosity is the source of that knowledge.

*Chapter 4*

# Curiosity and Leadership

. . . . . . . . . . . . . . . . . . . . . . . . . . . . . . . . . . . . . . . . .

If your actions inspire others to dream more,
learn more, do more and become more,
you are a leader.

*Simon Sinek, Leaders Eat Last*

. . . . . . . . . . . . . . . . . . . . . . . . . . . . . . . . . . . . . . . . .

THE NUMBER ONE question related to curiosity is, "Is there a correlation between curiosity and motivation?" The second most-asked question is, "What is the correlation between curiosity and leadership?"

Are successful leaders typically more curious than the rest of us? Is curiosity one of the secrets to better leadership?

According to most behavioral scientists and business leaders, the answer is an unqualified yes. While curiosity, many will say, does not ensure that a business leader will be successful, you won't find many successful business leaders who are not highly curious. In fact, many of them, including Microsoft founder Bill Gates, describe curiosity as one of the three Cs of successful leadership along with creativity and commitment.

Considering this emerging tenet, it might be surprising to learn that some leaders are reluctant to apply this principle. The thought is that curiosity is a distinction that separates excellent leaders from those deemed less effective. Those deemed less effective, research suggests, tend to avoid failing, being criticized, making hard decisions, taking responsibility, or being unable to reach an important goal. As a result, they may fear that their curiosity could expose them as not being as smart as they want people to believe.

Also, as a result, those leaders often surround themselves with individuals who are experts to compensate for their own lack of curiosity. Know anyone like that? That practice tends to inhibit them from developing curiosity skills on their own. Effective leaders, by contrast, appear to be comfortable in the space of the unknown, the uncomfortable.

The same curiosity that can be stymied by fears becomes the antidote for overcoming them. Deborah Bowie, CEO of Transforming Lives through Charitable Giving, stated, "The opposite of fear is not bravery, but curiosity. When we know more, we fear less."

But how do less effective or aspiring leaders develop curiosity? And how is that curiosity best expressed?

In addition to being a bestselling author and keynote speaker, Kevin Cashman is the senior partner for CEO and Executive Development at Korn Ferry, the world's leading executive search firm. He says the answers to those questions require simply "asking questions and listening."

When I interviewed Kevin, he stated, "Questions are the expressive, probing language; and listening is the receptive, facilitating language. Combined, these two behaviors are the key to leadership development." He continued, "Learning agility is more critical than IQ, and the foundation of learning agility is curiosity!"

Another dimension of curiosity, as Cashman cautiously pointed out, is that "Some people are more curious about themselves than curious about those they lead or how they can advance their team to the next level. That is not necessarily a good type of curiosity."

*   *   *

In a survey of more than a thousand CEOs, the majority cited curiosity and open-mindedness as leadership traits that are becoming increasingly critical in these competitive times.

One of the respondents, McCormick & Company CEO Alan D. Wilson, said, "The business leaders who are always expanding their perspective and what they know—and have that natural curiosity—are the ones who are going to be successful." Examine the attributes of a successful leader, he says, and you'll find curiosity at or near the top.[28]

In his weekly senior leadership meeting, GE President and CEO Jeffrey Immelt asked his leaders to reflect on the one leader who was most influential in their lives. He also asked them to cite the characteristic or behavior that made the influence strong. The answers varied, but they had one common theme. They said,

"He listened . . ."
"He was interested in my opinion on matters . . ."
"She sought my advice . . ."

"She made it a point to solicit thoughts from others . . ."

"He made me feel like I knew as much as he did . . ."

"He always solicited new thoughts and ideas . . ."

"Interesting," Immelt said in response to this feedback. "None of you cited attributes that suggested 'direction giving.' You all cited qualities of curiosity in others' opinions. That is our mission—not to direct but to seek new ideas."[29]

When asked to name the one attribute CEOs will need most to succeed in these turbulent times, Michael Dell, the chief executive of Dell, Inc., replied, "I would place my bet on curiosity."[30]

What's emerging is an era in which leaders are not expected to have all the answers; rather, they demonstrate a strong curiosity and propensity for asking questions. "Curiosity," Dell noted, "inspires leaders to continually seek out fresh ideas and approaches needed to keep pace with change and stay ahead of competitors."[31]

The famed Hollywood producer Brian Grazer wrote in his book, *A Curious Mind: The Secret to a Bigger Life,* "If you're the boss, and you manage by asking questions, you're laying the foundation for the culture of your company or your group."[32]

Grazer further stated that leading by curiosity can help to generate more ideas from all areas of an organization while helping to raise employee engagement levels.

Warren Berger, author of *A More Beautiful Question: The Power of Inquiry to Spark Breakthrough Ideas*, talked about the notion that curiosity can be good for business, an idea that's not entirely new. He said that Walt Disney declared that his company managed to keep innovating "because we're curious, and curiosity keeps leading us down new paths."[33]

While conducting research for his book, Berger uncovered numerous examples of leaders and CEOs (including Netflix's Reed Hastings, Square's Jack Dorsey, and the team behind Airbnb) who relied on a strong curiosity as the foundation for reinventing entire industries.

Berger told how Dorsey was curious to know why an artist friend lost a big sale to a potential customer simply because the artist couldn't accept a credit card. Dorsey disliked the fact that only established businesses, not smaller entrepreneurs, were able to conduct credit card transactions. That curiosity resulted in the creation of Square, a highly accessible credit card reader. He stated that "endless desire to explore new paths" becomes even more important in today's fast-changing, innovation-driven marketplace.

Dave Ulrich is known as the Father of Modern HR and HR Thought Leader of the Decade. He has written thirty books and more than 200 articles about leadership. In my interview with Dave, he talked about the power of soft skills and experimentation. He's also a strong advocate of "failing forward" and the importance of having curiosity not about the event itself but about the process leading up to the event. "What did we learn along the way about how we got here?" becomes the question.

Curiosity, it appears, is not only for start-up companies. Leaders of established companies, such as Panera Bread's CEO Ron Shaich, said curiosity is vital to surviving in a perpetually changing competitive landscape. "Every day, a new competitor arrives on the horizon, and every day it takes new ideas to retain whatever competitive edge you may have; even if they come from other industries, or even outside the business world."

So, if curiosity is such a vital element of effective leadership, why is it not more prevalent among leaders? The characteristic of curiosity is alien to traditional leadership norms. Many managers and top executives have risen through the ranks by providing fixes and solutions, not by asking questions. And once they've attained a position of leadership, they may feel the need to project confident expertise. To acknowledge uncertainty by wondering aloud and asking deep questions carries a risk; the leader may be perceived as lacking knowledge.

In *The Innovator's DNA*, authors Clayton Christensen, Hal Gregersen, and Jeff Dyer[34] studied curious, questioning leaders who seemed to overcome this risk because they had a rare blend of humility and confidence. They were humble enough to acknowledge that they didn't have all the answers and confident enough to be able to admit that in front of everyone else.

While we may tend to think of curiosity as a hard-wired personality trait, meaning that we are born with it, Ian Leslie, author of *Curious*,[35] said curiosity is actually "more of a state than a trait," and that we all have the potential to be curious but only under the right conditions.

Leslie noted that curiosity bubbles up when we're exposed to new information and then find ourselves wanting to know more. Hence, the would-be curious leader should endeavor to get out of the bubble when possible and to seek new ideas, influences, and experiences to fire up the desire for learning more and digging deeper.

Even when operating within familiar confines, curious leaders tend to see things from a fresh perspective. Those I researched seemed to have a penchant for bringing a beginner's mind approach to old problems and stubborn challenges. They continually examine and re-examine their own assumptions and practices. They also ask penetrating "Why" questions and speculative "What if" and "How" questions.

Curious leaders tend to urge people in their organizations to question everything. This can serve to model the behavior for others, though leaders may have to go much further by providing sufficient freedom and incentives to actually create the conditions for curiosity to flourish company-wide.

In the end, it isn't necessarily easy for a leader to foster curiosity on an individual or organizational level, but it may be well worth the effort. "With curiosity comes learning and new ideas," said Dell. "If you're not doing that, you're going to have a real problem."

Author and business consultant Michael Hvisdos, founder and CEO of Inquizos, a firm focused on customer loyalty, saw the paradox as a more systemic dilemma. He said, "I have worked with more than forty different organizations during the past few years that have embarked on a journey to transform the way they engage their customers. All made significant investments in retraining their customer-facing teams to engage differently, deliver value, and focus on *the one thing* their customers care most about: business outcomes. But not all have seen their investment bear fruit.

"Why should their levels of success be so variable?" Hvisdos continued.

"Countless business books have been written about this very subject. Whether it's organizational change or business strategy, almost everyone identifies the same reasons: business leaders typically do a poor job of leading change, be it due to competing priorities, lack of knowledge or poor application."

But if we know these reasons, why do leaders and their teams still struggle?

After analyzing a detailed study by Donald Sull, Rebecca Homkes, and Charles Sull published in the *Harvard Business Review*, "Why Strategy Execution Unravels—And What to Do About It," Hvisdos reduces the issue to one simple conclusion: many leaders lack curiosity.

He explained, "Simply defined, curiosity is, 'the desire to learn or know more about something or someone.' It is the starting point to every great idea, invention and new business. It is what makes some businesses wildly successful while others are just average, and it's the real reason why some leaders and their teams succeed, while others fail."

As Jeff Bezos put it, "You have to say, 'Wait a second. Why are we doing it this way? Could it be better? Could it be different?' That kind of curiosity, that explorer's mind, that childlike wonder, that's what makes an inventor."[36]

Leaders fail time and again to understand the situations, people, or customers they are engaging with because they simply aren't curious about them and feel more comfortable not leaving their comfort zones to find out.

Sull, Homkes, and Sull argued that organizations fail at execution because they don't adapt quickly enough to changing market conditions. Most leaders solve problems by trying to reduce them to single dimensions. And while that's true, what they really lack is more fundamental. They lack what the authors describe as "business curiosity."[37]

∗    ∗    ∗

### Business Curiosity

Thriving in a complex, volatile business environment requires leaders who approach every problem and every opportunity with an inquisitive spirit. This curiosity drives leaders to learn their companies inside and out. They never stop looking for ideas to improve.

This thirst for knowledge and wondering why enhances their ability to spot trends, anticipate changes, and tackle challenges. As Nolan Bushnell, co-founder of Atari and author of *Finding the Next Steve Jobs*, said, "Being able to problem-solve is more advantageous than just knowing the right answer.[38]

The phrase "business curiosity" continued to emerge in my conversations and research. Leaders and analysts alike consistently described the quality as continually asking why. Answers don't change the world, they say; questions do.

According to many who study successful leadership, business curiosity challenges leaders to question the very processes that made them successful and are used by their organizations and the customers they serve. Only when they question the very beliefs that made them successful can leaders start to reshape thinking, actions, and outcomes. It is then that they can start to capture and create more value for the businesses they lead.

In 2014, *Forbes* magazine contributor Micha Kaufman listed 10 Traits of Great Business Leaders. Six of these have direct ties to curiosity:

- Passion
- Vision
- Persistence
- Having an eye for talent
- Fearlessness
- Unwillingness to take no for an answer

The relentless pursuit to understand why allows you to think differently, learn from mistakes, and understand what makes people and organizations tick.

So again, why don't more leaders exhibit this critical trait?

As Hvisdos said, "Almost every business leader will say that one of the biggest challenges they face is managing time. Leaders get pulled in countless directions at a pace that would make a Formula One race feel like a Sunday afternoon stroll.

"But in reality, most leaders spend far too much time on low value, under-productive chores, which at best create only incremental value to the business and the teams they lead."[39]

Hvisdos went on to describe how many leaders devote their time to the many inward issues that sustain what he calls status quo thinking. This erodes their ability to exercise the curiosity that inspires new ideas that push their teams to new heights.

Mitch Little is vice president of worldwide sales for the semiconductor giant Microchip. He summed it up this way, "I think the biggest hurdle to developing curiosity is simply history and past beliefs. We have been groomed as leaders and sales people for generations to focus on our products, their benefits, their features, and the competition.

"Our legacy is the biggest impediment to our future. It is time to think differently! Once that legacy is understood and unleashed, the natural curiosity of our childhood can come out again. Leaders who purposely spend 60–80% of their time traveling and engaging with their team for months will be amazed what they will learn both about their team and about themselves."[40]

\*     \*     \*

Business curiosity (curiosity quotient or CQ) is not as widely studied as IQ and EQ, but as the *Harvard Business Review* article, "Curiosity Is as Important as Intelligence," discussed, people with a higher level of curiosity are more inquisitive and open to new experiences than others. They find novelty exciting and are quickly bored with routine. They tend to generate many original ideas and are counter-conformist.

The article noted that CQ is just as important when it comes to managing complexity. First, individuals with a higher CQ are generally more tolerant of ambiguity than those with a lower CQ. This nuanced, sophisticated, subtle thinking style defines the very essence of complexity.

Second, CQ leads to higher levels of intellectual investment and knowledge acquisition over time. Knowledge and expertise, much like experience, translate complex situations into familiar ones. Thus, CQ is the ultimate tool for leaders and their teams to devise simple solutions for complex problems.

Analysts, consultants, and business leaders alike remind me that although we are born with curiosity, we are not born leaders. Leadership skills must be developed.

They also remind me that the path to developing effective leadership skills is not IQ or even EQ, but CQ, the ability to retain the curiosity we exhibited as children. Successful leadership is derived by asking simple questions such as:

- "What if . . . ?"
- "Why do we do it this way?"
- "Is there a more efficient way?"
- "What do you think?"

Business today has evolved from the traditional militaristic, top-down leadership model referred to as Command and Control to a simpler, more engaging approach of Ask, Trust, and Track.

And curiosity has emerged as a vital leadership quality.

*Chapter 5*

# Curiosity and Engagement

. . . . . . . . . . . . . . . . . . . . . . . . . . . . . . . . . . . . . . .

Control leads to compliance;
autonomy leads to engagement.

*Daniel H. Pink*

. . . . . . . . . . . . . . . . . . . . . . . . . . . . . . . . . . . . . . .

THE TERM "ENGAGEMENT" could be misleading, especially in the context of this chapter.

Generally thought of as an individual's level of enthusiasm for their job, in this context, employee engagement is about one's emotional commitment to the organization and its goals. So then we ask:

- How engaged are we in our current jobs?

- How engaged are our employees in theirs?

- How committed are they to their company and its goals?

The questions don't stop there.

- What actions can we take to re-engage the unengaged?

- Why is the issue of employee engagement so important?

- What is the link between engagement and curiosity?

I launched our quest to understand the issue of engagement in the workplace in my interview with Kevin Sheridan, a leading consultant in the field of employee engagement and author of *Building a Magnetic Culture*.

Sheridan cited a Gallup survey that concluded that "Dis-engaged employees and turnover cost companies over $500 billion per year." According to Sheridan, that's the massive amount of money companies lose in the form of employee disinterest, lost productivity, attrition, recruiting, retraining, and other costs associated with employee disengagement every year.

Citing numbers from multiple studies and surveys, Sheridan categorized employees into three buckets: actively engaged, ambivalent, or actively dis-engaged. Then he stated that those in the ambivalent bucket constitute about sixty percent of our workforce with another fifteen percent in the actively dis-engaged bucket.

These numbers mean that roughly three quarters of the U.S. workforce is either marginally engaged or completely unengaged in their jobs and the growth of their companies.

Based on this assessment, America's workplace consists of more zombies than innovators and go-getters. Sheridan likens it to the walking dead.

\*   \*   \*

Consider the influence of another radio show guest, Doug Conant, former CEO at Campbell's Soup.

Doug's story is included in many of the courses I teach. He is credited with turning around a poorly engaged culture by doing a multitude of things, including writing personal notes. When I asked him if he wrote to all his employees, he responded, "We went back and did the math. I wrote ten to twenty a day, six days a week, religiously, for fifty-two weeks a year. We did the math and at a minimum, it was 30,000 notes to Campbell employees. It felt like more.

"Because we only had 20,000 employees, virtually everybody in the company had a note or two from me. That includes executive assistants and receptionists pinned in their cubicle or desk somewhere. I acknowledged something they'd done to help us move the company forward," said Conant.

Take a moment to reflect on your company's situation. Where do your employees fall on the spectrum of being fully engaged versus totally disengaged? What's the effect of these numbers on your company in lost productivity, attrition, recruiting, and training new employees?

What is the burden of your company's managers to motivate employees and keep them focused on the tasks at hand?

In 1996, with the automation revolution in its infancy, company leaders were preoccupied with things such as corporate reengineering and massive layoffs to improve productivity. This was noted in *The Loyalty Effect,* a book by Senior Consultant at the Bain Company, Frederick F. Reichheld.[41]

Reichheld wrote about working with a team of fellow

consultants to calculate the bottom-line effect of companies losing customers (over half in less than five years),
losing employees (more than half every four years), and
losing investors (roughly half every year).

Reichheld's objective was to calculate the cumulative
costs of those losses, to understand why they were
occurring, and to determine what could be done to
reverse such an alarming trend. He examined other
companies that were not experiencing those losses,
including Toyota Lexus, State Farm, USAA, Chick-Fil-A,
and John Deere. It became important to understand the
practices these companies used that made the difference.

What he found was engagement, practices to ensure
that a company's customers, employees, and investors
were actively engaged in the success of the company
and its employees. The practices uncovered that affected
levels of engagement included compensation and
related practices and benefits. But the causes went far
beyond these to include training, career development,
and recognition and retention practices.

Reichheld also discovered that corporate reengineering and layoffs had done little to yield gains in corporate performance. He concluded that the massive
disruptions corporations hoped would improve their
efficiency through their reengineering and layoffs had
the exact opposite effect on morale, attrition, and productivity.

In contrast, the author found that companies such

as the insurer USAA were achieving far greater yields than others by investing in their workforces. Employee training, career development, and recognition programs were cited as major factors that caused USAA to increase its productivity a hundred times with only a fivefold increase in its workforce.

Reichheld summarized, USAA "invests in employment and compensation policies that make their employees *want* to stay and produce."

Some twenty years after the initial publication of *The Loyalty Effect*, technologies have improved, and business practices have evolved and changed. Yet Kevin Sheridan, in *Building a Magnetic Culture*, cited the same formula that Reichheld found two decades earlier. The issue of poor employee engagement continues to separate top-performing companies from the also-rans.

\* \* \*

In today's world, exactly what is employee engagement, especially as the workplace continues its migration from the Baby Boomer culture to that of Gen Xers and Millennials?

Sheridan cited three simple factors:

1. Recognition
2. Career development
3. Employee relationships with supervisors

Millennials, Sheridan said, love feedback. They look for compliments regarding their work as many as twelve to fourteen times a day. Baby boomers climbed the corporate ranks in a very different time and culture. They neither expected that level of feedback in their own work nor do they feel compelled as managers to provide that feedback to their Millennial employees.

\*   \*   \*

> Appreciation is a wonderful thing. It makes what is excellent in others belong to us as well.
>
> *Voltaire*

"Suck it up," said Sheridan. If you cannot provide feedback to your employees fourteen times per day, you should at least target six to eight times a day. And it's not about being nice; it's about retaining talent and increasing productivity.

Sheridan also cited career development as being equally critical. Employees are eager to learn, grow, and expand their horizons, and the companies that provide a robust career development program will excel.

The third driver the author cited is the employees' relationship with their immediate supervisors. How many of us actively engage in our company's perfor-mance if we don't like the person we work for? Sheridan explained that this is not about the issue of likability; it's about human nature.[42]

Another proponent of employee engagement I interviewed is Dr. Bob Nelson. A consultant on the subject to literally hundreds of companies, he has authored twenty-nine books on the topic, including *1501 Ways to Motivate Employees* and *The Management Bible.* [43]

Nelson stated that the key to engagement is recognition. Echoing the same message as Sheridan, he said that employees (especially Gen Xers) look for constant recognition.

Similar to the sentiments Sheridan expressed, this practice wreaks havoc on many baby boomer managers who weren't trained to provide that level of constant feedback.

"Search for moments of positive achievements," Nelson advised, "even small achievements, and recognize them immediately. Tomorrow or next week is too late. You will have lost the moment. Delayed recognition could even have a negative impact."

The author went on to share stories and anecdotes that demonstrated the bottom-line virtues of employee engagement and teaming and cited his experiences characterized by the African proverb Embutu (*or Ubuntu*), roughly meaning, "I am because we are."

The 2008 world champion Boston Celtics embraced the same philosophy and even have the term engraved on their championship rings.

\*   \*   \*

### Management Practices to Attract and Retain Talent

Marcus Buckingham and Curt Coffman, management consultants for the Gallup Organization, conducted an extensive study to find the best management practices that attract and retain talent and achieve high levels of productivity. They ask questions such as, "Should a good manager be able to identify good talent? Or should a good manager be able to groom talent? What prevents employee attrition, better pay, or better management?"

Their massive study was conducted over twenty-five years and compiled into *First, Break All the Rules.*

Commonalities they found in high-performing managers were, first, they did not hesitate to break all the rules of conventional management practices, as the title of their book suggests. Second, they placed a great deal of emphasis on the care, well-being, and development of their employees.

Re-enforcing Sheridan's third driver that employees should have a close relationship and are liked by their co-workers, Buckingham and Coffman concluded:

> In today's tight labor markets, companies compete to find and keep the best employees, using pay, benefits, promotions, and training. But these well-intentioned efforts often miss the mark. The

front-line manager is the key to attracting and retaining talented employees. No matter how generous its pay or how renowned its training, the company that lacks great front-line managers will suffer.[44]

The authors further explained how the best managers select employees based on talent as opposed to skills or experience. Also, they:

- set clear expectations;
- define the right outcomes rather than the right steps or process to follow;
- motivate people;
- build on each person's unique strengths rather than trying to fix weaknesses; and
- find the right fit for each person as opposed to believing promotion to management is presumed to be the next rung on the organizational ladder.

Citing both corporate and individual performance metrics, Buckingham and Coffman concluded that the top-performing companies all excelled at employee engagement. They can determine an employee's commitment to their company by asking twelve key questions, such as, do I know what is expected of me at work? And, do my opinions count?

In 2018, a *Harvard Business Review* study revealed that while eighty-three percent of executives believe curiosity is encouraged at their company, just fifty-two percent of other employees feel the same way. Leaders who recognize this are more likely to encourage their teams to explore and less likely to make false assumptions.[45]

Kevin Kruse is another popular spokesperson on engagement and the author of multiple books on the topic, including *Employee Engagement.*

In my interview of him, he lauded the value of Buckingham and Coffman's work but concluded that twelve questions were too difficult for managers to remember. Instead, he sought to simplify the questionnaire. Working with researchers, he distilled the twelve questions into four.

1. Growth: Do my employees feel they are growing in their work?

2. Recognition: Are they being recognized for their work?

3. Trust: Do they trust that they and the company are on the right track?

4. Communication: Are there means by which to engage in those discussions?

Kruse cited simple, inexpensive examples of how to engage employees in these questions. He emphasized catching them in laudable or even coachable moments to cite their behavior and let them know they are valued. He said that employee engagement is neither expensive nor time consuming when done well.

Using these four questions, are your employees actively engaged in their work? If the answer is no, then what can be done to engage the ambivalent or the actively disengaged?

Sheridan *(Building a Magnetic Culture)* offered a sampling of three actions that could be taken:

- Volunteer them for assignments or committees.
- Mix them with workers who are actively engaged.
- Consider moving them into a role more suitable to their skill set, as they may be in the wrong job.

So, what is the relationship between engagement and curiosity? Simply stated, curiosity is the engine that propels employee engagement, by asking questions such as:

- How can I improve in my job?
- In what ways can I make this a better company?
- What are my competitors doing?

- What are the best practices in my industry?
- What do thought leaders say?

It is your curiosity that will help you find the answers to each of these questions. Curiosity leads to motivation, which leads to engagement.

How engaged are your employees? The answer lies in the question, "How curious are your employees about their work?"

I am engaged; therefore, I am curious.

*Anonymous*

*Chapter 6*

# Curiosity and Intelligence

. . . . . . . . . . . . . . . . . . . . . . . . . . . . . . . . . . . . .

Curiosity and creativity are intelligence
having fun.

*Albert Einstein*

. . . . . . . . . . . . . . . . . . . . . . . . . . . . . . . . . . . . .

WERE LEONARDO DA Vinci or Albert Einstein born brilliant, or did they acquire their intelligence because they were extremely curious? Are curious people naturally intelligent? Are smart people naturally curious? What, if any, is the correlation between intelligence and curiosity?

These are the questions that I confronted on this topic. So, as is my tendency, I went back to the beginning, aided by earlier work I'd done when studying intelligence and emotional intelligence during my doctoral studies. However, I knew there was more to learn in answering these questions.

For starters, here's what we know.

The words "intelligent," "intelligence," and "IQ" are as common to us as the words "smart," "genius," or "brilliant." Since childhood, it's been instilled in us that we're either smart or not smart.

Later in school, we took IQ exams to measure and prove just how smart we are. The words took on a social connotation, and in some instances, a social stigma. They could be an enabler or source of encouragement and motivation. Or they could serve as a barrier or inhibiter to what we could or could not accomplish in life.

Once the judgment of "not very smart" is bestowed upon someone, the expectations are automatically lowered for that individual, consciously or subconsciously. At one point in his life, Einstein was deemed not very smart, only to later be classified a genius.

This chapter offers some perspective on those words and assumptions in the context of the workplace and lifetime employability. We begin by briefly looking at the origins of the words and how they evolved to establish the connotations they have. Then for some, we'll proceed to demolish the assumptions attached to them.

We also look at early studies about intelligence and how our intelligence was viewed to be fixed—that is, unable to be developed or improved. We then examine how recent studies offer a new and different perspective and how one's intelligence can indeed be developed.

Finally, we attempt to put it all together. How can we use and develop those key elements of our intelligence toward the objective of sustaining lifetime employability?

### Intelligence and IQ

Picture your brain forming new connections as you meet the challenge and learn. Keep on going.

*Carol Dweck*

Since its early beginnings as the study of human behavior evolved, the term "intelligence" migrated from the realm of philosophy to become a central ingredient in psychology. Today, the study of intelligence has advanced significantly; however, psychologists are still debating its exact definition.

Despite differing views, scientists and behaviorists generally conclude its definition to be: The mental capability to, among other things, reason, plan, solve problems, think abstractly, comprehend complex ideas, learn quickly, and learn from experience.[46]

### *From Intelligence to IQ*

The term "intelligence quotient" (IQ) as the measure of one's intelligence was coined by a psychologist named William Stern while at the University of Breslau in Germany in 1912. Though there has been much refinement over the years, the IQ test, its scoring systems, and its standards for administering remain the standard for measuring intelligence.

Tests for IQ are designed not only to assess book learning (a narrow academic skill) or test-taking abilities, but also to assess an individual's broader, deeper comprehension of their surroundings. How well is that person able to understand a situation and effectively solve problems?

From the scoring and testing standards that have evolved, it appears that approximately two-thirds of the population score between 85 and 115; about 2.5 percent score above 130; about 2.5 percent score below 70.

In the earliest studies of intelligence, the subject of IQ was rather binary; a person was either smart or not smart. Since the IQ test was first introduced, intelligence has become more expansive in scope, but beliefs about it have largely remained the same. It was believed the intelligence you are born with is the intelligence you die with. Little could be done to change that fact.

With the IQ test, behavioral scientists continued with that rather simplistic view that intelligence was intelligence, and the IQ test was the measuring standard. You're either smart or not smart, and your IQ score told us how smart. Other attributes such as personality or talents were ancillary by-products of your intelligence. But your intelligence, scientists continued to believe, was a simple, straightforward calculus.

However, in the second half of the twentieth century, those views began to change.

### Fluid versus Crystalized Intelligence

In the 1960s, a British psychologist named Raymond Cattell put forth the proposition that intelligence took two distinct forms. The first is our foundational intelligence. That, Cattell said, equates to our base level knowledge, generally formed through our early learnings and experiences. We learned our ABCs, and we learned that 2 + 2 = 4. We learned that dogs can bite, and bees can sting.

That foundational intelligence, which relies heavily on past knowledge or learnings, is what Cattell referred to as "crystalized" intelligence.

Cattell then introduced a second type of intelligence that equates to our ability to grasp new lessons or new experiences, which he referred to as "fluid" intelligence.

Cattell, along with one of his former students, John Horn, conducted further research and wrote a series of publications on fluid versus crystallized intelligence. Their work changed several earlier beliefs on the subject.

Their work was also instrumental in destroying another earlier theory that intelligence could not be developed. That belief was dramatically changed when they conducted a variety of studies demonstrating that fluid intelligence could indeed be developed.

Those studies put the subject of intelligence in a brand-new light.

### *Types of Intelligence*

To take the analysis of intelligence a step further, in the 1980s, a psychologist named Howard Gardner led a series of studies to examine other elements of our intellect. He studied things such as talents and special abilities, which were traditionally viewed as traits ancillary to intelligence. He determined that those traits were different forms of intelligence.

Just because someone is not good at math, Gardner concluded, it doesn't mean that person isn't intelligent. Intelligence comes in different forms or specialties, he said. In 1983, he wrote of nine different types of intelligence, including elements now associated with emotional intelligence, such as interpersonal and intra-personal intelligence.

With Gardner's work, the concept of intelligence was no longer binary; it was multidimensional. To add to the topic's growing complexity, scientists began to dissect the IQ test itself, to look at the true measure and behavioral meaning of one's level of intelligence. If someone is regarded as smart, what differentiates that person from someone who's regarded as *really* smart?

### Building Blocks of Intelligence

Considering that intelligence is multidimensional, are there elements that underlie or support all types of intelligence?

Let's get to the question at hand: what is the correlation between intelligence and curiosity, your IQ and your CQ (curiosity quotient)?

Having intelligence is clearly important to academic performance. But, like so many other ingredients for achieving success in life, intelligence is necessary but not sufficient.

Everyone knows of a brilliant kid who failed school or someone with mediocre smarts who made up for it with hard work. That's why research psychologists are looking at factors other than intelligence that make some students do better than others.

One element is conscientiousness, that is, the inclination to go to class and do the required homework. People who score high on this personality trait tend to do well in school.

Sophie von Stumm from the University of Edinburgh in the UK is coauthor of "The Hungry Mind: Intellectual Curiosity Is the Third Pillar of Academic Performance."[47] She stated, "It's not a huge surprise, if you think of it, that hard work would be a predictor of academic performance."

von Stumm and her coauthors concluded that curiosity is another important factor. "Curiosity is basically a hunger for exploration," stated von Stumm. "If you're intellectually curious, you'll go home, you'll read the books. If you're perceptually curious, you might go traveling to foreign countries and try different foods."[48] Both of these could help students do better in school.

The researchers performed a meta-analysis, gathering the data from about 200 studies totaling about 50,000 students. They found that curiosity did, indeed, influence academic performance. In fact, it had quite a large effect, about the same as conscientiousness.

Combined, conscientiousness and curiosity had as big an effect on performance as intelligence. von Stumm wasn't surprised that curiosity was so important. She explained, "I'm a strong believer in the importance of a hungry mind for achievement, so I was just glad to finally have a good piece of evidence. Teachers have a great opportunity to inspire curiosity in their students, to make them engaged and independent learners. That is very important."[49]

Employers may also want to take note. A curious person who likes to read books, travel the world, and go to museums may also enjoy and engage in learning new tasks on the job.

"It's easy to hire someone who has done the job before and, hence, knows how to work the role," von Stumm said. "But it's far more interesting to identify those people who have the greatest potential for development, the curious ones."[50]

> Don't just teach your children to read. Teach them to question what they read.
>
> *George Carlin*

Abraham Maslow, the famed psychologist who was best known for creating Maslow's hierarchy of needs and the concept of self-actualization, stated that "Fear of knowledge . . . is a protection of our self-esteem, of our love and respect for ourselves."[51]

If we can learn a love for knowledge, we can grow

and learn to love ourselves and, with courage, love and master our environments. Therefore, parents should be shown the positive effects of supporting their children's curiosity and how to best do so. School curricula could first focus on teaching kids an intrinsic desire to know before feeding them facts.

The authors of a 2011 study published in *Perspectives in Psychological Science* found that curiosity is a big part of academic performance.[52] According to the study, personality traits such as curiosity seem to be as important as intelligence in determining how well students do in school. In fact, as Einstein said, "Curiosity is more important than intelligence."

In another study, scientists from the Samuel Lunenfeld Research Institute of Mount Sinai Hospital in Toronto discovered a molecular link between intelligence and curiosity. This could lead to the development of drugs that will improve a person's ability to learn.

Dr. John Roder, senior investigator at Lunenfeld-Tanenbaum Research Institute, and Bechara Saab, PhD candidate at Lunenfeld Institute, studied the interaction of two proteins in a small region of the brain called the *dentate gyrus,* part of the hippocampus, which plays a role in long-term memory and spatial navigation. They published a paper on this in 2009 in *Neuron.*

For the study, the neuronal calcium sensor-1 (NCS-1), a protein known to affect the memory of worms, was linked to bipolar disorder and schizophrenia in people.

It was increased 150 percent specifically in the dentate gyrus of mouse models. This modest over-expression increased the ability of brain cells to change how they communicate with each other. In effect, it gave the mice superior memory in complex tasks and a significant increase in exploratory behavior (curiosity).

Because the exploratory behavior was only altered in safe environments, the researchers concluded that they had discovered a region of the brain that generates and enhances curiosity. It becomes a model for how brain activity directly leads to curiosity. These researchers also discovered that both curiosity and spatial memory were impaired when blocked by certain drugs.

Wrote Bechara Saab, "Now that we know that some of the molecules and brain regions that control learning and memory also control curiosity, we can go back to the lab and design drugs that may improve cognition in humans. That's the potential benefit for the future. Immediately, however, we can put into use the knowledge that fostering curiosity should also foster intelligence and vice versa."[53]

So, we now know that curiosity is not the exclusive domain of the intelligent, but curiosity can increase our intelligence. Just ask Einstein.

*Chapter 7*

# Curiosity, Creativity, and Innovation

- - - - - - - - - - - - - - - - - - - - - - - - - - - - - - - - - - - -

Curiosity is the engine of achievement.

*Sir Ken Robinson*

- - - - - - - - - - - - - - - - - - - - - - - - - - - - - - - - - - - -

THROUGHOUT MY CAREER as a behavioral expert, assistant professor, and speaker about human behavior, individuals and students have asked this question: "Are curiosity and creativity the same thing? And if not, how are they related?"

Given the frequency of the question and the intensity of the discussions that have followed, and given that this book is about curiosity, I feel compelled to address this question.

Creativity or innovation is perhaps what CEOs seek most in their employees. Innovation is the key to competitive advantage, which is the key to survival. Today's product is only as good as tomorrow's newer and better version. How many times have we heard analysts ask, "When will Apple introduce a newer version of its iPhone?" Yes, today's product is yesterday's news. We want to know what's next.

To better understand the link between curiosity and innovation, I researched work by Gregory Mirzayantz, an author, blogger, and all-round commentator on the human condition. (Get ready for a mind warp and an intellectual game of Twister.)

When asked "Are curiosity and creativity the same

thing?" Mirzayantz used his best deductive logic and posed this response:

> If curious people are always creative, but creative people are not always curious, then curiosity drives creativity.

> But if curious people are not always creative, and creative people are always curious, then creativity drives curiosity.

What does that trail of inquiry have to do with curiosity and innovation? Perhaps Leonardo da Vinci concluded that it was his pervasive curiosity that drove him to his many creations manifested in his masterful paintings and sculptures. Many of today's corporate leaders and consultants agree that this approach remains true today.

Joe Calloway, a business author, consultant, and speaker whose clients range from Coca-Cola and Verizon to Cadillac and American Express, said, "I really believe that curiosity is like a muscle that must be used in order to stay strong."

Mike Federle, CEO of *Forbes*, said, "Add something unexpected to your regular routine. Walk a different route to work, study a subject of which you think you have little interest, examine your inner voice, and understand the narratives you create about yourself."

Scott DuPont, of the DuPont family, said, "Keep a pen and paper handy or the voice recorder on your smart phone and capture the thoughts that come to your mind—those you are curious about and may want to explore!"

Mark Sanborn, professional speaker, entrepreneur, and author of the best-seller *The Fred Factor: How Passion in Your Work and Life Can Turn the Ordinary into the Extraordinary*,[54] described this approach to creativity and innovation: "I am one of those people who is interested in many things. I believe creativity comes from reading, experiencing, and learning outside your field. If you're in a cafe in a new city, don't take refuge in your cellphone. Watch the people around you and notice little things about them: how they interact, how they use their bodies when they speak, and whether they take their time or exude a sense of hurry. Once you connect with the present, breathing and noticing instead of seeking distraction, your judgments and fears will lessen, and your curiosity will blossom."

> Position yourself with something that captures your curiosity, something that you're a missionary about.
>
> *Jeff Bezos*

To get out of this mind-twisting labyrinth and closer to understanding the relationship between curiosity and innovation, I introduce you to Faisal Hoque. Hoque is a serial entrepreneur and the founder of Shadoka, a firm dedicated to creativity, entrepreneurship, and innovation. He is also the author of *Everything Connects: How to Transform and Lead in the Age of Creativity, Innovation, and Sustainability.*[55] In his book, he wrote, "Experiences are the fuel of creativity; and curiosity is the thirst which drives those new experiences."

Aha! This clarifies the issue. It all begins with our curiosity. Curiosity then leads us to experiences, and those experiences then lead to creativity. So, according to Hoque, it is curiosity that drives our creativity.

When I interviewed billionaire entrepreneur Jeff Hoffman, he stated the same thing. "As we get older, some people just lose that natural childlike curiosity about the world around them. What I started to notice is the world's greatest innovators never do . . . lose that sense of childlike wonder."

Psychotherapist Diana Pitaru takes the view that the relationship between creativity and curiosity is symbiotic. She said that the two must work hand-in-hand, that is, without one (curiosity), you can't have the other (creativity). Thus, if our creativity heavily depends on our curiosity, then where would original and valuable ideas come from if curiosity didn't exist?

Albert Szent-Gyorgyi has some insight. This Hungarian biochemist won the Nobel Prize for discovering vitamin C and the components and reactions of the citric acid cycle. He said, "Discovery exists when you look at the same thing as everyone else and think something different. That isn't easy." He was known to have loved the scene in the movie *Dead Poet's Society* when Robin Williams' character climbed on his desk and asked his students, "Why am I standing on my desk? I stand upon my desk to remind myself that we must constantly look at things in a different way."

Innovation many times comes from the least likely sources. England's Great Ormond Street Hospital, which treats heart patients, was experiencing an inordinate number of casualties when patients were being transferred from one unit to another. One of the physicians was watching a Formula One race and was particularly impressed by how quickly and efficiently the pit crews serviced everything, mistake-free, in seven seconds or less.

So, he invited Formula One racing teams to come in and view the hospital's transfer procedures, and then make observations based on their own procedures. The three-step process recommended by the racing teams, once implemented, reduced the hospital's errors by more than 50 percent.

Toyota, the Japanese car manufacturer, constantly looks to its employees for innovation. It expects them to offer as many as 100 suggestions a year on how to improve processes. Similarly, Google allows up to twenty percent of an employee's time to be dedicated to curiosity and innovation. Each of them, like the Formula One pit crews, believe that by focusing on the small things, the big things take care of themselves.

Adam Markel, an international speaker and author of the best-seller, *Pivot*, said on my show, "If you want to be an innovator, either in your business or in your personal life, you've got to be willing to take small steps every day. Not big leaps, but small steps."

Larry Robertson echoed the same theme in *The Language of Man: Learning to Speak Creativity*. He wrote, "Creativity requires a willingness to reconsider even the most well-worn or deeply cherished assumptions."[56] (We will discuss this idea further in Part III.)

\* \* \*

> If necessity is the mother of invention, then curiosity is its father.
>
> *Rupal Bhadu*

Now let's throw innovation and invention into the mix.

When we hear "Necessity is the mother of invention,"

that assumes someone created something to fill a need in society. In Jared Diamond's Pulitzer Prize-winning book *Guns, Germs, and Steel: The Fates of Human Societies,* he explained that many times this is not always the reason for inventions. "In fact, many or most inventions were developed by people driven by curiosity."[57] Even Edison didn't initially consider the phonograph to reproduce music.

Innovation is at the top of many leaders' lists for what they'd like their staff members to improve in their organizations.

To be innovative means to come up with new methods, ideas, or products. That requires asking questions and challenging the status quo. There must be a strong desire to learn something new. The trick is how to develop that desire in people.

As we age, our natural sense of curiosity becomes a less dominant force. How can we explain that? There are a multitude of reasons, including (to name a few):

- Fear of failure
- Assuming we know things we don't
- Technology doing things for us
- Others suppressing our natural desire to explore and learn

If we want people to be curious at work, we must recognize what holds them back. How can we expect them to solve problems if we don't allow them to ask questions? How can we anticipate receiving innovative ideas if we micromanage their time and interests?

Many employees don't provide input for fear of looking stupid. Yes, we can tell them that there's no such thing as a stupid question. But if our actions don't align with our words, they'll keep their questions and ideas to themselves.

The most innovative companies encourage employees to share their passions and ideas. Companies such as Facebook, Uber, Amazon, and Google recruit employees who ask questions. As Google's CEO has said, "We run this company on questions, not answers."[58]

To improve innovation at work, we need to lead by example, ask questions, and demonstrate empathy based on what we hear. We must avoid groupthink, promote learning, and reward natural curiosity. We recognize this requires persistence to ensure that we don't quit when we run into the unexpected.

Yes, we can embrace what we don't know by creating an environment that rewards curiosity and crazy questions. If we observe leaders such as Elon Musk (Tesla), Sir Richard Branson (Virgin Airlines), and Sergey Brin and Larry Page (Google), we see that they explored new areas and broke through boundaries.

How can we expect our people to explore new boundaries and create innovation if we as leaders tie their hands?

> Even if your ambitions are huge, start slow, start small, build gradually, build smart.
>
> *Gary Vaynerchuk*

### Big Innovative Breakthroughs

Instead of looking at innovators as not following the rules or being contrary, we need to consider that crazy questions have led to big innovative breakthroughs. So we don't get placated into believing we have all the answers, we need questions such as:

- "Why not?"
- "Why doesn't this work?"
- "What are we missing?"

Rather than rewarding conformity, again we need to examine what make us hold onto it. We require brutal honesty, investment in training that brings out our natural sense of curiosity, and allowing people to create stretch goals outside what feels comfortable.

Instead of relying on technology to solve our problems, let's occasionally put technology aside and consider what we don't know about what technology can do for us. Are we getting only superficial answers when there's more to explore if we simply asked questions?

We need to question ourselves as well as our employees. We might assume that we know the answers to things we don't even understand. We must resist the desire to remain where we are, and instead look ahead to the possibilities.

To do that requires being humble, confident, self-aware, and realistic. We can embrace nonconformity and collaboration, resisting a need to control everything. If we hold ourselves back by telling ourselves we are shy or a team player, that won't produce out-of-the-box thinking. Rather, let's ask open-ended questions that require critical thinking, and then listen carefully to what we hear in response.

If we focus on others rather than ourselves, that is a big step. After all, we tend to see the world from our own stories. What if we could live in someone else's mind to see things from a fresh perspective? What new ideas could our two conjoined minds bring out?

Yes, working on our inner monologue could be a big first step. We can stop telling ourselves that we aren't creative or that other people are better at coming up with things. If we see the fun involved in learning and exploring, we could be an integral part of the innovative process. If we get out of our routines and change our environment, that could spark some new ideas.

Simple things like looking up a new word a day or writing a blog about something we don't know could open our minds to something never conceived.

Spending time around diverse environments to see things from another perspective can be crucial. Let's surround ourselves with people who have done bigger things. They help us see things from a "been there and done that" perspective and can remove the taboo or fear of exploration.

We must look at failure as a learning experience and part of the process rather than as a problem. Only then can we get people to venture out of the safe zone. When we create motivational moments, we ignite emotion and improve our sense of well-being.

How has your organization gone about rewarding those who ask questions, challenge habits, and seek adventure?

> Much of what I stumbled into by following
> my curiosity and intuition turned out
> to be priceless later on.
>
> *Steve Jobs*

\* \* \*

In 1941, Georges de Mestral, a Swiss engineer, was hunting with his dog in the hills of Switzerland and became annoyed when he returned home to find his clothes and his dog covered with burdock burrs. After spending hours removing the unwanted burrs, he was curious to know the quality that gave the burrs their ability to cling to clothing, fur, and other objects that passed their way.

He put one of the burrs under a microscope to examine the phenomenon more closely. He discovered that the surface of the burrs consisted of tiny hooks that could attach to any object that provided a receptive surface. That receptive surface included anything that provided a loop, such as clothing, hair, or animal fur.

de Mestral was struck by the burrs' exceptional sticking characteristics and pondered how he could apply this concept and replicate that sticky characteristic. After several experiments, he thought of creating a fabric to be used as a product fastener based on the principles of the burdock burr. He concocted a name for the fabric by combining the French words "velours" (velvet) and "crochet" (hooks). He called the fabric Velcro.

Reflecting on Faisal Hoque's formula, we see that de Mestral had an experience that led to curiosity, which resulted in his creation.

John Bessant, professor of innovation and entrepreneurship at the University of Exeter, has cited great discoveries of our time that occurred by accident and curiosity. Through the inventors' perseverance and curiosity, experimental failures became game-changing innovations. Here are some examples:

A melted chocolate bar in Percy Spencer's pocket inspired a product we use every day. While working on microwave-based radar equipment for the defense contractor Raytheon in 1945, Spencer noticed that, when activated, the technology melted a chocolate bar in his shirt pocket. His curiosity took over. After a myriad of experiments, the microwave oven was born.

In the 1930s, Kutol Products was a struggling company trying to sell its paste to clean the soot residue from coal-fired stoves and off of walls and furniture. By the 1950s, coal-based heating was becoming obsolete and so was Kutol as a company. But children, as unintended users of the cleaning solution, discovered a more lucrative use for the cleaner and saved the company. The new product was called Play-Doh.

In the 1930s, Roy Plunkett was a chemist working on chlorofluorocarbons for the chemical giant, DuPont, to improve refrigeration materials. When he returned to examine his latest experiment, he was disappointed to find that one of the canisters no longer contained the gas he had hoped for. It had a waxy build-up instead. His curiosity provoked him to further experiment with materials, and he discovered the extraordinary lubricating qualities it was able to provide, even at high temperatures. The result was the product called Teflon.

The list could go on to include products such as

Viagra, Super Glue, penicillin, and Silly Putty, all born from a curiosity that defied failure and disappointment.

## What If . . . ?

Creativity demands having an open mind, which seems to be the common thread for all the inventors, entrepreneurs, and successful business leaders we've examined. And all those individuals asked the same question: "What if . . . ?"

Sometimes, they asked a variation of this question, such as "I wonder what happens when . . . ?" or "I wonder what you would get if you did A and B?"

Creativity is questioning the familiar or having the desire to pursue the unknown. Whether it's painters trying new blends of color, gardeners experimenting with hybrid plants, or dog breeders testing new breeds, curiosity provokes a variation of the question "What if . . . ?" while providing the fuel that leads to creation.

## The Virtues of Failure

Accompanying the mixture of curiosity and creativity is a dramatic reduction in the fear of failure.

Have you ever been so focused on creating a piece, repairing a machine, or solving a problem that you ignored every failed experiment along the way? You just kept on going until the problem was solved. Your failures were completely overridden by your determination. Think about how many times you said, "Well, that didn't work. What if I do it this way?"

> I have not failed. I've just found 10,000 ways that don't work.
>
> *Thomas Edison*

Behaviorists tell us that the combination of curiosity and the pursuit of a creation or a solution is the antidote to the fear of failure. Whether we're creating an invention or solving a problem, when we're focused on the solution, we don't dwell on the failures along the way. We just keep trying until it's done.

Michael Gelb is an internationally renowned author and speaker on curiosity and creativity. Among other features, he conducts an online class, *How to Think Like Leonardo da Vinci.* He said, "By nature children are curious, but as we grow up much of our inquisitiveness ebbs. Almost all children in their natural state ask lots of questions. That's how they learn so much in the first five years of life. But then we send them to school where they learn that answers are more important than questions. Creative geniuses like da Vinci, however, maintain that passionate curiosity throughout life, which results in a lifetime of creativity."[59]

Innovation, or creativity, appears to be the by-product of curiosity, which may entail many failures along the way to sometimes surprising success. CEOs are well served to foster both curiosity and innovation and take the failures in stride because many times they're worth the result.

*Chapter 8*

# The Curiosity of the Successful

........................................

There is no better catalyst to success
than curiosity.

*Michael Dell*

........................................

FOR DECADES, WE have been hearing about the strong link between successful leaders and curiosity. I've had the privilege of interviewing many of those successful leaders on my radio talk show. All have extolled the virtues of curiosity as being integral to their success. Practitioners and scientists are at odds over many of the factors that contribute to success, but on this issue, they seem to agree.

*Psychology Today* stated that the top trait among those who succeed is curiosity. A common characteristic is that successful people read to satisfy their curiosity. They like to explore new things and are open to fresh ideas. They constantly ask questions and seek information to fulfill a voracious appetite for knowledge. They want to learn everything about everything.

> Give people facts and you feed their minds for an hour. Awaken curiosity and they feed their own minds for a lifetime.
>
> *Ian Russell*

When Warren Buffett was asked about the key to success, he pointed to a stack of books and said, "Read

500 pages of this every day. That's how knowledge works. It builds up, like compound interest. All of you can do it, but I guarantee not many of you will do it."[60]

Buffett reads between 600 and a thousand pages a day. Bill Gates reads fifty books a year, and most are about business, science, and engineering. Mark Zuckerberg claims to read a book every two weeks. Mark Cuban claimed that he will try to read three hours a day if he needs to learn something new. Elon Musk said he read the entire encyclopedia when he was only nine years old. Oprah reads so much, she created Oprah's Book Club.[61]

*Inc.* magazine devoted an article to how many of these successful people dedicate five hours a week to deliberate learning, called the five-hour rule. They see learning as being so crucial to success that not spending the time to learn leads to insidious long-term effects such as having an unhealthy lifestyle. The article states, "The CEO of AT&T makes this point loud and clear in an interview with *The New York Times*; he says that those who don't spend at least five to ten hours a week learning online 'will obsolete themselves with technology.'"

There are certain famous people who come to mind when we think of successful people who are curious. *The Irish Times* listed Sir Hans Sloane, a physician born in 1660, as the most curious man in the world, due to his interest in collecting objects from his worldly travels. Others who read to satisfy their curiosity include Einstein, Disney, Aldous Huxley, Madam Curie, Richard Feynman, and Malcolm X. The list is endless.

When I asked Marshall Goldsmith, a world-renowned business educator and coach, about how to leverage curiosity and success, his response was interesting. He said, "The nice thing about being around a hundred coaches is it's just a great way to learn. To me, when you are around someone who does something that's like what you do but not exactly like what you do, it's very good because they are all so smart. You're not competing in any way. You're just helping each other."

*　*　*

To cultivate curiosity, it's important to recognize moments when the situation requires powerful open-ended questions to obtain meaningful information.

Unfortunately, many people hesitate to ask questions at work. A *Harvard Business Review* article found that sixty-five percent of employees do not believe they can ask questions at work, even though eighty-four percent of them said that their employers encouraged curiosity.[62] That is a curious contradiction. Perhaps it's because sixty percent of them believed there were barriers to question asking in their workplace.

Michael Bungay Stanier, senior partner of Box of Crayons and author of *Do More Great Work*, has urged people to find a favorite opening question and practice it and practice it until it becomes a habit. He said his favorite go-to question is, "And what else?" because the first answer stated is never the only answer.

A common topic in the business courses I teach examines Abraham Maslow's Hierarchy of Needs. Maslow popularized the term "self-actualization," which is the desire for self-fulfillment and realization of our full potential. He studied people he believed reached self-actualization, including Abraham Lincoln, Thomas Jefferson, and Einstein.

Later in his career, Maslow regarded this actualization as less of a peak and more of a disciplined event that we teach ourselves through experience. He found that self-actualized people embraced both the unknown and the ambiguous.[63]

> Everyone shines, given the right lighting.
>
> Susan Cain, *Quiet*

Author Adam Bryant interviewed 700 CEOs for his book *The Corner Office: Indispensable and Unexpected Lessons from CEOs on How to Lead and Succeed*. He asked them, "What qualities do you see most often in those who succeed?" Their number one answer was passionate curiosity.[64]

This characteristic, passionate curiosity, is seen as a survival mechanism because our involvement in life depends on our interest in it. Buddhists often call this willingness to cultivate a sense of wonder a "beginner's mind." People with that mindset become lifelong learners.

As Elizabeth Gilbert, author of *Eat, Pray, Love*, said, "Curiosity-driven people bring the gift of cross-pollination to every space they occupy."[65]

The more we begin to see what is possible, the more likely we are to figure out how to attain lifelong learning. What we strive to achieve can always be greater. As Steve Jobs said, "Those crazy enough to think they can change the world usually do."

So, just what's different about the curiosity of the successful business leaders we hold in high esteem and our own curiosity?

I asked that question of Jeff Hoffman, the billionaire entrepreneur instrumental in creating Priceline.com. He said, "I ask the same question. I ask what it is they're doing that everybody else is not. What is common? What are the common traits and behaviors of those people?"

Jeff explained, "I love to be around people whose accomplishments I admire, as I did on a trip to the UK with Steve Wozniak (Woz), co-founder of Apple. The whole time Woz and I were traveling, I noticed the same trend, stopping to pick up shiny objects and asking, "What is that?" And you're thinking, "Who cares? We're in the middle of something.""

Yet the successful people do care. They wonder what

something is and how it works. Then they want to take it apart and see what's inside.

Theirs is a thirst for constant learning. They want to know more, they want to know why, and they want to know how. They're likely to be great innovators because they stumble upon things nobody else even looked at before.

> There will always be someone who can't see your worth. Don't let it be you.
>
> Mel Robbins, *The 5 Second Rule*

Todd Kashdan is an often-quoted professor at George Mason University in Fairfax, Virginia, and leading researcher on the topic of curiosity. He stated, "On the surface, curiosity is nothing more than what we feel when we are struck by something novel."[66]

Kashdan has published *Curious? Discover the Missing Ingredient to a Fulfilling Life,* in which he outlined the benefits of cultivating a curious outlook.[67] He explained how we tend to dismiss curiosity as a childish, naïve trait, though knowing it can actually give us profound advantages.

Curiosity is the trait that helps us approach uncertainty in our everyday lives with a positive attitude.

"Although you might believe that certainty and control over your circumstances bring you pleasure, it is often uncertainty and challenge that bring the longest-lasting benefits," explained Kashdan. "In part, I think it's because it's easy to lose sight of what truly sustains us, and where the true meaning in our lives should come from."[68]

But putting curiosity at the heart of everything means that we experience daily life by discovering the unfamiliar in the familiar, as Kashdan put it.

Discovering the unfamiliar in the familiar seems to be a major differentiator that separates moderately successful people from those who appear to enjoy success at an altogether higher level. They not only appear to see things differently from the rest of us; they appear to see the same things differently every day.

Do the ultra-successful possess some form of super-curiosity? The answer is no. They just tend to find the unfamiliar within the familiar. As Louis Pasteur said, "Chance favors the curious mind."

In the *Huffington Post,* Kira Callahan, an expert sales conversion coach in the financial industry, explained how successful sales people use their curiosity. He said, "Curiosity is the fuel behind the world's great achievements and discoveries. Genuine curiosity lights a fire between people that is the foundation for mutual respect and lasting relationships."[69]

> Be curious, not judgmental.
>
> *Walt Whitman*

### *Discovering the Unfamiliar in the Familiar*

While researchers and behavioral scientists pursue the Holy Grail of Curiosity and its variations and what differentiates the super successful from the rest of us, my research brings me back to this single concept: discovering the unfamiliar in the familiar.

I know the route from my home to the grocery store very well. I drive it several times each week. And each time, I take the same route. That's the familiar. What if I occasionally took a different route? Might I find it to be shorter or more convenient? Might I discover interesting new people or new businesses worth exploring? What else might I notice taking a different path to that same old destination?

For anyone who has worked in the same job for a year or more, we are prone to fall into that rut of familiarity. We are susceptible to that dreaded disease called burnout.

What if, instead of answering those predictable phone calls with a predictable response, we changed it up?

What if, instead of going into that sales call on automatic pilot with the same proposition, we observed a customer's behavior we'd never noticed before and asked the person to explain it?

What if we observed that assembly line that we oversee every day from the perspective of a child and asked, "Why?"

To find the unfamiliar in the familiar, the examples are endless. For some, a particular idea may seem difficult to do, even a little ludicrous. To the super successful in the world, however, it's second nature.

*Chapter 9*

# Curiosity and Age

. . . . . . . . . . . . . . . . . . . . . . . . . . . . . . . . . . . . . . . .

Old age begins when curiosity ends.

*Saramego*

. . . . . . . . . . . . . . . . . . . . . . . . . . . . . . . . . . . . . . . .

D OES OUR CURIOSITY change as we age? Does it decrease? Do we lose our childlike curiosity as we grow? Do Millennials tend to have more curiosity than Baby Boomers, or less? Is age a factor in determining our curiosity to learn new things or to pursue new ideas? Just curious!

According to Robert Stokoe, director of the Jumeirah English-Speaking Schools in Dubai, United Arab Emirates, "Three-year-olds, on average, ask their parents about 100 questions a day, every day! However, by the time they are ten to 11 years of age they've pretty much stopped asking. Of even greater concern is that by the age of 25, only two percent can think outside the box. Curiosity seldom survives childhood. Adult creativity is still powerful, but there is just not enough of it. It can be said that the creative adult is the curious child who survived."[70]

Dr. John Bowlby, a famed psychoanalyst who conducted a wide range of studies on curiosity and age, concurred with Stokoe. However, his acknowledgment included a qualifier.

Best known for his child attachment theory, this psychoanalyst wrote that intuitive curiosity found in young children can be greatly influenced by their mother or caregiver to whom they become feverishly attached. "Secure infants," Bowlby stated, "who view their caregiver as a secure base, feel safe to explore their environment, knowing they have that secure environment. Insecure infants, on the other hand, who do not feel the safety and security of their caregiver, are far less inclined to explore their environment."[71]

Carol Dweck, author of *Mindset: The New Psychology of Success*, described the phenomenon in simple, binary terms. Children are greatly affected by their caregivers in terms of putting the child into either a growth or fixed mindset.[72] Dweck described the language that tends to encourage a growth mindset, phrases such as "Let's find out," "I wonder," and "What if . . . ?"

> Every mind is born with the instinct of curiosity. We all come into the world curious, an innate gift which newborns demonstrate as soon as they are born when they begin to look around.
>
> *Robert Stokoe*

In light of Bowlby's qualifier, if we take Stokoe's article at face value, our curiosity is indeed strongest as a child but tends to lessen as we age. If you've ever played iPad games with an eight-year-old who is catching on more quickly than you are, you might tend to agree.

*   *   *

Then there is the dreaded fourth-grade slump.

Educators describe a phenomenon in which children between the end of the second and the middle of the fifth grade show a declining interest in reading and studies in general. Some say they're developing interests in video games, organized sports, and other after-school activities. Others say our education system tends to overwhelm them with tests and other assessments. By the fourth grade, the pupils feel burned out.

This phenomenon may be more of a commentary on our education system than on childhood development. As one educator said, "By the fourth grade, kids go from learning to read to reading to learn."

Research has shown that our brains go into the beginning stages of decline as early as our mid-twenties. But does that decline include curiosity as well? In 2014, the Public Library of Science published a study designed to answer that and related questions.

Researchers had 3,305 volunteers ranging in age from the mid-teens to the mid-forties play a video game called StarCraft 2, which required quick thinking and real-time strategy. The objective of the study was to gauge whether we begin to rely more on our experience and less on our curiosity as we age.

The researchers began the study with the premise that we employ our experience to compensate for our age-related decline, creating what they called "over-the-hill intuition." Do our brains begin to slow down as we age, therefore causing us to compensate by relying more on our experience?

This game required the participants to make a myriad of dynamic adjustments as they executed a game plan. While each player performed a variety of tasks, they were also required to form a long-term strategy.

The results from this game were both predictable and surprising.

The researchers concluded, "The speed with which the volunteers made decisions and shifted between tasks definitely declined with the older participants, with the first signs of cognitive decline beginning around the ripe old age of 24."[73]

> I could not, at any age, be content to take my
> place by the fireside and simply look on.
> Life was meant to be lived. Curiosity must be kept
> alive. One must never, for whatever reason,
> turn his back on life.
>
> *Eleanor Roosevelt*

That research concluded that there was cognitive decline as we aged but showed no decline in curiosity. Related studies have suggested that while our brains may experience decline as we age, our curiosity remains intact and may actually increase. That appears to be particularly true when confronted with topics that may not have interested us as children.

For example, when I was young, I had no curiosity or interest in anything related to history or social studies. However, visiting Pearl Harbor as an adult, I became more interested in learning about the Pearl Harbor bombing in 1941 and related events in ways I would not have earlier.

It appears that as we travel the journey into adolescence and adulthood, our curiosity tends to narrow from the wide-open spaces of our childhood to topics of more specific use or interest. They might include education, parenting, career, hobby-related issues, or even history. But the research continues to emphasize that positive re-enforcement and a supportive learning environment remain essential parts of that journey from childhood through old age.

Psychologist William Herbert Sheldon said, "There are those rare people who never lose their curiosity, their almost childlike wonder at the world. Those are people who continue to learn and grow intellectually until the day they die. And they are usually the people who make contributions, who leave some part of the world a little better off than it was before they entered it."[74]

Continuing the search for connections between curiosity and age, psychologists Rhenna Bhavnani and

Corrinne Hutt of the University of Reading conducted a study to track the growth in curiosity of boys and girls, as they grew from age seven to age nine. The study was published in the *Journal of Child Psychology and Psychiatry*.[75] It exposed different groups to curiosity-laden topics to see if the added exposure affected lasting curiosity and creativity over a two-year period.

While the study did not reveal significant changes in girls as they aged over that time span, it did demonstrate that boys showed significantly higher levels of creativity when exposed to novel stimuli.

Given that previous studies have shown that mothers display a stronger interest in and connection to their daughters than their sons, it's speculated that other factors may have influenced the study. The lack of significant increases shown by the girls in the study could be attributed to the extra levels of exposure provided by their mothers that the boys did not get.

Exposure. That seems to be another important key in maintaining our curiosity as we age. Stated Bowlby, "We tend not to be curious about that to which we have not been exposed."

I strived to expose my own children to everything I could, even if I had no personal interest in the subject. As I write, I've had flashbacks of sitting in the stands on cold nights watching my daughters play softball. I had absolutely no interest in watching softball, especially on cold nights. But I wanted them to experience sports, as well as the arts and academics. Without exposure to several of these, they wouldn't know what might interest them.

*   *   *

> The greatest invention in the world is
> the mind of a child.
>
> *Thomas Edison*

From young children to older adults, the connection between curiosity and age continues to remain intertwined.

Becky Thomas, an author and executive coach who works extensively with generational issues in the workplace, has pointed out factors in the curiosity of different age groups.[76]

Thomas's work has echoed the same theme of John Bowlby's studies with children, adding that the opposite dynamic can also occur as we grow older. The lack of safety can enhance one's curiosity.

Thomas explained, "The safety and security an individual feels about their surroundings is clearly a factor regarding curiosity more than a person's age. But consider that Millennials grew up in a time with very low trust, due to the Financial Crisis, the events of 9/11, parents losing their jobs, etc. So, because they have low trust, they're apt to question things at a higher rate than a Gen Xer or baby boomer would at their age. Earlier generations grew up in a very 'safe' era and typically trusted leadership, so there wasn't the questioning and curiosity in the same way there is now."[77]

Thomas continued, "Curiosity is also heavily tied to the value the individual places on learning. Millennials, or young professionals, are possibly more curious because they are still seeking to learn about issues their older counterparts already know. But, overall, the *safety of the environment* and the *value the individual places on learning* tend to be stronger variables than age in determining one's curiosity."[78]

\*   \*   \*

Going one step further, researchers Gary Swan and Dorit Carmelli conducted a study that showed, as we age, curiosity can add to the longevity and quality of our lives, up to thirty percent longer and a higher quality of life.[79]

The study, funded by the National Institute of Aging, examined the curiosity levels among nearly 1,200 white men averaging age sixty-five. It also factored in physical health risks, including blood pressure, cholesterol level, and history of smoking, cancer, depression, or stroke. The subjects were followed for five years to see if curiosity had any differentiating effects on the length or quality of their lives.

The results showed a strong correlation between curiosity and strong physical and psychological health. They were not startling, but the strength of the correlation between the two was surprising.

After separating out the physical variables, the men who showed higher levels of curiosity were thirty percent more likely to live beyond those five years than the men with merely average curiosity. A related study of more than a thousand women found similar results.

Why would higher levels of curiosity relate to better survival in older adults, the researchers were asked? They explained that higher levels of curiosity can provide an improved ability to respond to the challenges of aging, such as limited mobility or changes in living arrangements.

"Those with higher levels of curiosity showed better coping skills with new challenges or new experiences. They were also more adept at establishing new friendships and showing new ways to solve problems. The adaptive value of exploratory, problem-solving behavior is fundamental to living longer."[80]

The researchers concluded: "When we are children, our curiosity leads to effective intellectual and emotional development. When this child-like trait continues, it enhances our ability to live longer with more active lives."

"Conversely," they continued, "shrinking curiosity may be one of the earliest signs of abnormal aging of the central nervous system, an added health risk and a possible contributor to the shortened life span."

Dr. David Larson, epidemiologist at the National Institute for Healthcare Research, commented on the study: "Previous studies have shown that a spiritual outlook can lengthen the lives of the elderly. This study indicates that curiosity is connected to longer life as well."[81]

Contrary to what many people believe, it appears that curiosity does not diminish with age. As we are reminded, curiosity is an intrinsic trait, just as is our need for food and water. It remains with us throughout our lives. Curiosity does, however, become more discriminating as we age. The curiosity of children is wide open; they show interest in anything about everything. They're discovering life experiences for the first time, and nothing is out of bounds. As we age and learn, we become more selective about our interests.

Chances are, at some point in your childhood, the metamorphosis of a caterpillar into a butterfly intrigued you. Unless you are a zoologist, though, chances are you're no longer curious about that phenomenon.

From the child who is curious about everything, to the college student whose education depends on becoming curious about trigonometry, to the retiree who, for the first time in his life, becomes curious about Social Security, the thirst remains. It is only a matter of what you drink, or if you choose to drink at all.

Imagine children as bundles of curiosity with an innate desire to discover the world around them. Now imagine shutting off or discouraging that natural tendency.

The loss of curiosity is not a function of aging but a learned fear of knowledge.

# Chapter 10

# Curiosity and Emotional Intelligence

. . . . . . . . . . . . . . . . . . . . . . . . . . . . . . . . . . . . . . . . . . . . . . . .

Emotional intelligence accounts for
80 percent of career success.

*Daniel Goleman*

. . . . . . . . . . . . . . . . . . . . . . . . . . . . . . . . . . . . . . . . . . . . . . . .

D OUG CONANT DESCRIBED the occasion when he lost his job and engaged an outplacement agency in his pending job search. He said the agency greeted him with what he described as four magic words that transformed his attitude and ultimately his leadership style, "How can I help?" Those four simple words, he said, served as a touchpoint. It became a cornerstone for how he engaged disenfranchised employees and increased profits during his tenure as president of Nabisco and as CEO at Campbell's Soup.

In this brief vignette, Conant exhibited what is commonly referred to as emotional intelligence (or EI) for having the awareness and sensitivity to realize the impact people's emotions have on their day-to-day performance and the curiosity to delve into the unknown and sometimes murky waters of those emotions.

The combined qualities of curiosity and its relationship to emotional intelligence are a subject that has intrigued me even longer than the subject of curiosity itself. Much of my doctoral work placed a major emphasis on EI, and throughout my studies, I found the two behaviors consistently described as having a close, almost symbiotic relationship.

So, in this chapter, I propose to first define and clarify

exactly what is (and what is not) emotional intelligence and then to examine how emotional intelligence relates to curiosity.

First things first: just what is emotional intelligence?

That question may not be as simple as it seems. EI is sometimes confused with the term emotional quotient or EQ, which is the measurement of EI. The two terms can easily be confused. Further, even those who are viewed as pioneers in the study of emotional intelligence all seem to take a slightly different view on the subject.

For example:

Some of the earliest studies of EI were conducted by psychologists Peter Salovey and John D. Mayer. In their work, the two established that emotions enhance one's pursuit of productive outcomes when properly directed, which was in stark contrast to earlier theories of intelligence, which posited that emotions tend to impair logical thought or reasoning.

In their article "Emotional Intelligence," published in 1990, the two professors defined the concept as "the ability to monitor one's own and others' feelings and emotions, to discriminate among them and to use this information to guide one's thinking and actions." [82]

Their work was considered groundbreaking in the way they dissected the concept of EI into three categories:

1. how one assesses and communicates their emotions;

2. how one can manage or regulate their emotions; and

3. how one can effectively apply their emotions in the way they interact with others.

Their work is instrumental in defining EI and establishing the relationship between EI and a wide range of behaviors deemed critical to success, from creativity to leadership.

Another pioneer in the study of EI is psychologist, author, and science journalist Daniel Goleman. Though heavily influenced by the findings of Salovey and Mayer, he formed a somewhat different view on the subject. He has authored several books on the significance of emotional intelligence and has been an ardent champion of the notion that our emotions play just as critical a role in our success as does our intelligence. Goleman is largely credited for taking the work of Salovey and Mayer beyond the research lab into the mainstream.

In his definition of emotional intelligence, Goleman described EI as having these five components:

- Self-awareness: Our ability to know ourselves, good and bad, and to be comfortable with that knowledge.

- Self-regulation: Our ability to control disruptive impulses and to think before acting.

- Internal motivation: Our ability to pursue goals with energy and persistence.

- Empathy: Our ability to understand the emotional makeup of other people.

- Social skills: Our ability to build and manage relationships and networks.

Beyond the scientific analyses of EI, I was most interested in the laymen's view and how EI and curiosity combine in that symbiotic relationship I spoke of previously. What do the authors, motivational speakers, business leaders, and entrepreneurs say about the two?

From the perspective of a business leader, Garry Ridge, president and CEO of WD-40, said it this way: "You mentioned emotional intelligence. Probably the biggest reason that I've seen most people who are very smart fail as leaders is because their ego eats their empathy instead of their empathy eating their ego."

Another recent guest on my program, Professor M. S. Rao, offered a similar perspective. Rao is known as the father of soft leadership and founder of MSR Leadership Consultants in India. He said, "Mostly overlooked, soft skills play a large part in actually keeping one's job. While people are hired for their hard skills like knowledge, oftentimes people get fired for their lack of soft skills, including their emotional intelligence."

Kare Anderson, an Emmy-winning former NBC and

*Wall Street Journal* reporter and a guest on my program, took the question to an even deeper psychological realm: "We need to keep reminding ourselves that what makes us feel anxious, fearful, slighted, or otherwise stressed can have a deeper and longer tug on our attention than what makes us feel happy. Remind yourself that when you find a reason to feel good, in the moment, you can become more observant and able to make smarter choices, learn more and deepen connection with those you are around."

However, from whichever vantage point you view the subject, the numbers don't lie. *Forbes* reported that forty-six percent of newly hired employees will fail within eighteen months. A lot of that is attributed to miscommunication, interpersonal skills, and soft skills, including emotional intelligence.

People typically don't lose their jobs because they can't do the work. They lose their jobs because they can't do the work with other people, whether it's colleagues, supervisors, subordinates, or customers. Personality clashes are not a function of intelligence as much as they are a function of emotional intelligence.

Simon T. Bailey is a public speaker, author, life coach, entrepreneur, and author of *Shift Your Brilliance: Harness the Power of You, INC.*[83] He laid the topic out in very sobering terms on my show: "There are two different spectrums. There are leaders who are narcissistic and unfortunately will not keep their employees for very long. Then there are leaders who are tapping into that deeper emotional area. They are becoming very self-aware. To borrow a little bit of your work and your dissertation around emotional intelligence, they are becoming aware of their areas where they have failed because whatever you don't deal with will eventually deal with you."

Guy Winch, psychologist and author of the bestseller, *Emotional First Aid: Healing Rejection, Guilt, Failure, and Other Everyday Hurts*,[84] offered his view about the universal nature of EI: "When we experience emotional wounds like rejection, failure, or loneliness, we're not even aware that these are emotional wounds that need to be treated. Why it resonated with people is because everyone has emotions, and everyone was like, 'Yes, I have those feelings.' Maybe that's correct that we do need to do something about them. Across cultures, languages, age, gender and races, EI is a characteristic that affects us all."

Kevin Surace, an American technology innovator, speaker, and entrepreneur, made the differentiation between EI (or EQ) and IQ. When I interviewed him on my show recently, the CEO of Appvance, creator of an AI-based software QA platform, and *Inc.* magazine's 2009 Entrepreneur of the Year, answered this way: "Google has dumbed us down because Google will just answer all those questions. Arguably today, Alexa can do the same thing just by asking many of those questions.

We're no longer curious about trivia questions; we just answer them. It's no longer useful for the human mind to spend any time on it.

"'Can AI help us with X?' is a curiosity question in Silicon Valley today. Often the answer is no. Everyone to your left and everyone to your right has about the same IQ plus or minus ten points. So, your IQ is not what's going to determine if you can become a CEO. Chances are, everyone is as smart as the next person, so that's not the determining factor. What differentiates them is EQ, which they're not taught it in school, in college, or at work."

Of all of the guests who have appeared on my program to discuss curiosity and emotional intelligence, perhaps none have done so with as much animation and enthusiasm as Naveen Jain.

This billionaire, entrepreneur, and philanthropist explained the interdependency of EI and curiosity with great passion. He described intellectual curiosity as the key to solving both elementary problems at home and the problems of the world.

Jain, the founder of Moon Express, Viome, and other firms, also said, "Don't lead a horse to water; make him thirsty, and he will find the water on his own."

Okay, so we've heard from the scientists, the entrepreneurs, the authors, and the motivational speakers. But what about the tough guys, I mean, the *really* tough guys. How would they view the importance of soft skills, including emotional intelligence? Would they characterize EI as being critical to leadership?

I was determined to find out, so I talked with Mark Divine, a Navy Seal and expert in human performance. He emphasized mental toughness, leadership, and physical readiness. You would think his would be the consummate macho-based program with little or no focus on what we call soft skills. But I'll have to say, he surprised me when I interviewed him.

When I asked him about the significance of EI in his leadership program, he said, "It is the power of your whole mind that makes a profound impact on the decisions you make and on your quality of life . . . that is the combination of your emotional intelligence, visual intelligence, imagination, visualization, and your intuitive intelligence. Much to the contrast of what many people believe, EI is an essential quality of toughness and leadership."

I guess soft skills don't make anyone soft. According to Divine, it's just the opposite.

> Emotional intelligence is not about being nice.
> It is about being impactful.
>
> *Anonymous*

There is a wealth of knowledge regarding the importance of developing curiosity. Researchers have concluded that curiosity, especially trait curiosity, has a positive relationship with emotional intelligence. Kashdan, Rose, and Fincham found that curiosity positively affects "motivation associated with recognition, pursuit, and self-regulation of novelty and change."

So, according to the behaviorists, the scientists, the business leaders, the entrepreneurs, the motivational speakers, the authors, and even the Navy Seals, if you are in the position of engaging others, EI appears critical. And yet again, it is curiosity that serves as its engine.

\* \* \*

Okay, so we know EI is important, but what if you don't have a high level of emotional intelligence? How can you tell? Are there specific behaviors that indicate you may be lacking in EI?

Muriel Maignan Wilkins, co-founder and managing partner of Washington, D.C.-based leadership coaching and consulting firm Isis Associates, described the telltale signs of an absence of EI:

- People often become impatient or frustrated when others don't seem to understand them.

- They feel people are too sensitive and overreact to their comments.

- They are generally unconcerned with being liked at work.

- They weigh in early with their beliefs and defend them with rigor.

- They have the same expectations for others as they apply to themselves.

- They tend to blame others for most of the issues on their team.

Based on his ten years as an executive coach, Wilkens stated, "I have never had someone raise his hand and declare that he needs to work on his emotional intelligence. Yet I can't count the number of times I've heard from other people that the one thing their colleague needs to work on is emotional intelligence. This is the problem: Those who most need to develop it (EI) are the ones who least realize it."

So, given those behaviors, do you have sufficient emotional intelligence?

> No one cares how much you know,
> until they know how much you care.
>
> *Theodore Roosevelt*

\* \* \*

Through my own studies and countless interviews, I have always viewed the traits of curiosity and emotional intelligence to be essential soft skills, but I must admit that I had not fully appreciated the true nature of their connection until researching this book. Neither did I fully appreciate how the two, when working together, serve as anchor points for what many behaviorists perceive to be the Holy Grail of human behavior: achieving a meaningful life.

Let me conclude this section of my treatise on curiosity and its significance to so many critical aspects of our lives with a summation by Tomas Chamorro-Premuzic. He is an organizational psychologist, a professor of business psychology at University College London and Columbia University, and CEO at Hogan Assessment Systems.

In his 2014 publication, *Managing Yourself*, he mused about the age of complexity in which we find ourselves.[85] He noted the vital nature of what he views to be the three key psychological qualities that will best serve us in our ability to survive: IQ, EQ, and CQ.

Chamorro-Premuzic stated, "While IQ is not something that can necessarily be taught or coached, EQ and CQ can indeed and *must* be developed if we are to thrive as business professionals, leaders or entrepreneurs."

The author concluded: "Curiosity is the ultimate tool to help us produce the solutions we need to solve the complex problems we face."

# PART II
## *Roadblocks*

*Chapter 11*

# What Holds Us Back?

· · · · · · · · · · · · · · · · · · · · · · · · · · · · · · · · · · · · · ·

Those with less curiosity or ambition just
mumble that God works in mysterious ways.
I intend to catch him in the act.

*Damien Echols*

· · · · · · · · · · · · · · · · · · · · · · · · · · · · · · · · · · · · · ·

NOW WE GET to the heart of what I've wanted to know about curiosity: what holds us back? Why do some people retain their curiosity to solve perplexing problems, invent new technologies, or discover new worlds while others become less curious? Answering that question is my mission.

We usually recognize incurious people when we encounter them, much the same way we recognize the immature or unintelligent. They may be our children, our students, our fellow workers, or even ourselves. But how do we confront them? Do we simply tell them that they're incurious and to snap out of it?

When confronted with motivating the seemingly unmotivated, psychologists and behavioral scientists suggest a first step. First, break the concept down into specific behaviors. Then, rather than correct the person, correct the behavior.

When I looked up the word incurious in the dictionary, I found a variety of synonyms I expected, such as apathetic, casual, complacent, and disinterested. So far so good. However, I also found two words that had completely escaped my vocabulary up until then: insouciant and pococurante. Like the punchline of a joke or the ending of a story, the meanings of these two words made me—guess what—curious.

"Insouciant," according to Webster's, is an adjective that means being "free from concern" or "anxiety free." Hmm, I remember my children being insouciant about math, which led to grades that were not their best.

"Pococurante," I discovered, is an adopted Italian word meaning "a careless or indifferent person." When I was an MBA Program Chair, I never realized I had pococurantes (or pococuranti) enrolled in the program. Neither did I know that pococurantism was so prevalent among high schoolers.

Other definitions describing the incurious are more familiar, such as nonchalant, perfunctory (another good one, meaning lacking interest or enthusiasm), unconcerned, indifferent, or uninterested.

Beyond expanding our vocabularies, we can now better determine the specific behaviors associated with the incurious by learning its various definitions. For example, what do people do or not do when they are apathetic or uninterested? Remember, experts say that once we know the behaviors associated with being incurious, we're better equipped to change their state.

*     *     *

To further this quest, let's go back to the basics of curiosity discussed in Chapter 1. We discussed how curiosity is innate to all of us and grounded in the notion of survival or finding food and shelter and being protected from predators.

Scientists tell us that all mammals have a limbic system within our brains. Designed to trigger memory, emotions, and arousal, the limbic system is the basis of our survival instinct. Before we continue our analysis of the incurious in humans, let's briefly examine curiosity where it's more vividly displayed, as in a few of our favorite creatures, beginning with cats.

Cats are in a continual state of curiosity. Even domestic cats maintain this inherent trait based on survival instinct. Felines aren't necessarily more curious than other animals. They just tend to exhibit their curiosity more visibly and in a more entertaining fashion. If you're a cat lover or study the behaviors of cats, you know what I mean.

Cats live in a constant state between curiosity and caution, exploring the territory but always remaining vigilant. It's like our own feeling of caution and impending danger when we almost fall over backwards in a chair. That's the world of cats, at least when they're not napping.

Dogs are just as curious as cats for the same survivalist reasons, but they cultivate and display their curiosity in different ways. Long possessing the title "man's best friend," dogs, like cats, are what zoologists call an altricial species. That means they're born blind and deaf and therefore totally depend on their mothers for their early survival. The opposite of altricial is precocial, which refers to animals that are largely independent and mobile at birth, such as horses or cows. (No charge for the extra lesson in zoology.)

The state of being altricial tends to enhance animals' curiosity. From the moment they're born, unable to see or hear, they almost immediately search for their sustenance and protection. This helpless condition appears to serve as an early catalyst for their curiosity and survival.

Ever watch dogs during a walk in the woods or the park? They sniff everything, whether it's humans, plants, or other dogs. Their highly developed sense of smell and their equally keen sense of hearing are their primary means of satisfying their never-ending curiosity.

Have you ever subjected your pet to a laser pointer and watched it madly chase the dot of red light? That's another behavior of dogs and cats that's not only entertaining but an example of their strong curiosity. Does this behavior mimic that of trying to catch prey? What seems like mindless fun to us is an element of the survival instinct they possess.

Monkeys display similar entertaining and curious behaviors. Cats, dogs, and monkeys all exhibit the innate nature of curiosity, grounded in the instinct to survive. There's no such thing as an incurious cat or dog or monkey. They retain their survivalist instincts even when they're domesticated.

That incurious distinction belongs to us humans. Why? When we evolve beyond the state of survival, we allow our curiosity to diminish.

> You can't just give someone a creativity injection. You have to create an environment for curiosity and a way to encourage people and get the best out of them.
>
> *Sir Ken Robinson*

But it doesn't start out that way. Babies are born learners with a natural curiosity to figure out how they can survive and how the world works. Curiosity is the desire to learn, an eagerness to explore, discover, and figure things out.

Parents and caregivers don't have to make infants curious or push their toddlers to learn. In fact, research shows that it's an internal desire to learn and not external pressure that motivates them to seek out new environments to explore.

Watch babies as they follow sounds, faces, and interesting objects with their eyes. Notice as they shake a rattle and then put it into their mouth to see what this object can do and what it tastes like.

As babies age and figure out more and more of how the world works, their curiosity fades or becomes more focused or directed. Somewhere along the line, however, some people remain curious and others do not.

Why is that?

Beyond any physical or health-related factors that can dampen our curiosity, such as stress, dementia, or drugs, research leads to four major factors that impede or diminish this quality in humans. I've labeled these factors FATE (fear, assumptions, technology, and environment).

### #1 Fear

Based on testing, fear is the most predominant factor that influences our curiosity. It may be fear of the unknown, fear of what we might find, fear of the uncomfortable, or fear that the results of our exploration might challenge our current beliefs.

Fears are sometimes disguised as false bravado or ego. Fear of failure tends to be major. How many times have we threatened to quit our jobs or wanted to start a business fearing what will happen if it doesn't work out?

Our curiosity rarely gets the chance to explore the options of a new job or how to start a new business before the dreaded "yeah, buts" shut it down. Our fear overtakes our courage and curiosity.

The desire to try something new or different is fruitful only when our determination or motivation to explore further or learn more mitigates the risks we feel anxious about.

The more curious we are, the more we come to know. The more we know, the less fearful we become. The inverse of that is also true. The less we know, the more fearful we are and the less we come to know.

How does fear inhibit your curiosity?

### #2 Assumptions (The Way Things Have Always Been Done)

Another common reason we become averse to trying something new, or even wondering about it, is that we get comfortable doing things the way we've always done them, or we consider the issue already solved. If we assume something already works, why explore something new or different?

In the business world, for example, speed is a virtue, and innovation is risky and expensive. Therefore, it's common for leaders to push for a fast and safe solution rather than a new, untried one.

One of the biggest paradoxes in industry today consists of holding on to tried-and-true solutions yet yearning for innovation. We might tell ourselves that we don't have time to exercise our curiosity and explore new ideas. However, as the world progresses and becomes more innovative, those who don't proactively seek new information won't keep pace. It's important to reward people for exploring new ideas and asking questions.

In our personal lives, we might select jobs based on what we assume is expected of us. Perhaps people in our family have always been engineers, lawyers, doctors, and the like. Therefore, we might think that we should pursue the same kind of path. Perhaps we tell ourselves that we must be good at a particular career or a certain line of work because that's what our lineage did.

Traditionally, we gravitate to the assumption that "if it ain't broke, don't fix it." However, the pace of innovation and entrepreneurship today suggests a new version of that expression: "If it ain't broke, break it!" Then, fix it and make it better than it was before.

What assumptions do you hold that might be preventing curiosity and innovation?

### #3 Technology

The third major factor that affects our curiosity is technology.

Technology has offered us so many answers and made it so much easier to access those answers, yet as generations become more and more technology dependent, curiosity can actually be squelched. If computers can answer our questions, we may not see the need to discover the why behind those answers.

So, technology can, in fact, dissuade us from learning new things. If learning something requires first trying out technology to discover answers, people can feel overwhelmed. For example, those who want to learn more about writing but have little knowledge about computers and online documents might be stymied.

Thus, they might not pursue their writing interest due to the sheer number of steps required.

Then there's artificial intelligence (AI). As it becomes more popular, we'll have more devices doing more things for us, requiring us to do less. Scientists have reminded us that the more we're given answers, the less likely we are to ask questions.

Thus, we have another of the paradoxes regarding curiosity as it relates to the emergence of technology: how do we sustain our desire to ask questions in a world more and more dominated by answers?

Can you look past answers to find more questions that may lead to breakthroughs?

### #4 Parental, Family, Teacher, and Peer Influence (Our Environment)

The fourth major category of factors that tend to suppress our curiosity is the environment in which we live or were raised. Social pressures can stifle our instincts to be curious.

Our families and friends might inadvertently put ideas in our heads that something isn't appropriate or is even bad because they fear the unknown. Sometimes having a friend join you in a curious endeavor can help alleviate that tendency to judge.

Social media have caused a lot of people to share only things that will be "liked" by other people. They might subconsciously worry that showing interest in something other than what everyone else has interest in will make them look bad.

Regarding education, it's a widely held belief that children are born curious and become discouraged in school. Sir Ken Robinson's widely popular TED talk asks the question: Do Schools Kill Creativity?[86]

As we age, we're told to act certain ways, which can inhibit curiosity and creativity. Learning environments can have a dampening effect. Teachers might inadvertently confine students to the curriculum, stifling a natural form of curiosity that might lead in a completely different direction. Researchers have even found that curiosity can be diminished if opposite-sex siblings occupy the same room.

Younger generations have begun to feel even more pressure to conform than other generations. Research indicates that Millennials are the most stressed-out generation. They lack risk tolerance when it comes to financial decisions and have less distress tolerance in the workplace. Because they worry about what others think of them more than other generations do, they're less likely to propose new ideas and speak up in meetings.

The lessons we learn from our parents, teachers, professors, and bosses are the same lessons that can stifle our curiosity later in life.

Were you taught only answers or also taught to question?

*   *   *

Boundless research on curiosity assures us that we are born with it, and it serves to acclimate us to the world around us.

We know that our curiosity leads to better performance and creativity and is essential to motivation and innovation. Curiosity is seen by entrepreneurs and business leaders around the world as making the fundamental difference between being good and being excellent. It's a key difference between surviving and thriving and between mediocre employees and outstanding employees.

To know how to instill curiosity, we must first know what gets in the way. We do know several factors that tend to curtail our curiosity, ranging from mental or physical impairments to laziness. We've added more clarity and specifics regarding those inhibiting factors of FATE.

In the following chapters, we'll explore the barriers within each of those four categories and how companies can remove them to unleash the potential of their workforce, which is our ultimate goal.

*Chapter 12*

# Curiosity and Fear

. . . . . . . . . . . . . . . . . . . . . . . . . . . . . . . . . . . . . . . . .

Curiosity is what draws you out of your comfort zone; fear is what draws you back in.

*Marc Jacobs*

. . . . . . . . . . . . . . . . . . . . . . . . . . . . . . . . . . . . . . . . .

F EAR, THE FIRST and most prominent of the four factors of FATE, is fully capable of blocking our curiosity, our pursuit of innovation, and our competitive advantage. Fear takes many different forms: dislikes, biases, opinions, and even bravado. But don't be confused; each of these is a variation of fear, and each can bring us to a paralyzing halt. That "deer in the headlights" sensation affects more than just deer.

A part of our brain, the amygdala, signals any signs of threat or danger we may encounter. Such detection triggers the release into our bodies of large doses of chemicals such as adrenaline and cortisol. While this function is essential to our survival, the amygdala has no ability to distinguish a real threat from an imaginary one. It doesn't know if we've confronted a bear or misplaced our iPhone. As Jason Ma, founder, CEO, and chief mentor of ThreeEQ, said when he was on my show, "It just knows our thought was negative, which provokes a fight-or-flight reaction within us."

For example, your amygdala remembers and stores in your brain the reaction you experienced in the third grade when you failed to answer the teacher's question. It remembers how your colleagues looked at you when you made an off-the-wall suggestion, and it reminds you that the last time you attempted a three-point shot at the buzzer you missed.

Whereas your amygdala may be essential in warning you that spiders and snakes can be a threat, it can also put a damper on your curiosity and desire to explore new things.

> The only thing we have to fear is fear itself.
>
> *Franklin D. Roosevelt*

Fear, at its core, is a reluctance to delve into the unknown. The reasons for that can range from the sublimely ridiculous to the deadly serious. They include fear of failure, fear of making life-altering mistakes, fear of looking stupid or ignorant, and even fear of re-experiencing something negative from our childhood.

To this day, I resist certain vegetables because as a child I found them to be disgusting. The script in my head goes something like this, "I ate cooked carrots as a kid and remember them tasting mushy and nasty; hence, I no longer want to try new vegetables." If you asked if I'd be interested in learning a new way to cook carrots, I must confess the answer would most likely be no.

Sally Helgesen, a noted consultant and author of *The Female Vision*,[87] noted recently on my show, "A big fear that women, especially, share is that you'll disappoint the expectations people have of you and that they'll say, 'That's so unlike her.'"

The fact is, any fear, however ridiculous it seems, is completely capable of impeding our curiosity and innovation. Fortunately, most of our fears aren't an impenetrable wall but are often like fragile panes of glass that can be shattered or overcome with a single action.

The term "fear" is defined as being overly cautious or reluctant to act to avoid consequences. In many instances, our fears are imaginary, something we anticipate could happen or might happen as opposed to what likely will happen. Insurance companies hire actuarial analysts to calculate the risks and probabilities of potential threats or occurrences. If something seems too risky, we tend to shy away from it.

Behavioral scientists and leadership coaches suggest the opposite. They encourage us to move toward the risk, not shy away. They remind us that a key difference between exceptional leaders and others is their high comfort level with delving into the unknown, exploring the uncomfortable.

Fear, in evolution, has a special prominence: perhaps more than any other emotion it is crucial for survival.

*Daniel Goleman*

*   *   *

Recently, I was swimming laps at my gym. By the side of the pool was a woman with her toddler. As small children tend to do, the child kept tugging at her mom to go toward the pool, only to be held back by her protective mother.

Eventually, the mother decided to let the child experience the water. Jumping in, she extended her arms to the child, urging her to jump. Repeatedly, the child excitedly ran up to the edge of the pool, but each time, she stopped just short of leaping into her mother's arms. After several aborted attempts, the exasperated mother got out of the pool and led her daughter away.

The infant was clearly curious to experience the sensation of being in the water, but her fear of the unknown overcame her curiosity.

How many times have we, too, been curious to experience something unknown or to explore a new opportunity yet were too fearful of what might result if we followed through? Generally, we don't fear physical harm, but rather we fear the risk of other kinds of discomfort.

To determine if fear is holding you back from discovering areas you might otherwise want to explore, ask yourself exactly what you fear. Is it the process or the outcome? Do you not believe you're capable of doing a particular task or job? Do you need more information to make a decision? What's at stake if you make a decision?

If you're considering writing a book, do you fear having it scrutinized or judged? What if you consider doing something but are told it's risky or scary? Would you accept this input at face value or explore what you want to do anyway?

What if you tried something and failed? Do you think you would look bad from someone else's viewpoint? Are you worried about being overwhelmed with too much to do? Or worried you'd be putting all your eggs into one basket?

> Our fear of failure tends to grind off our enthusiasm for risk taking and for entrepreneurship. We should be more in touch with what we get from our failures.
>
> *Tom Kolditz*

Consider how you would deal with your answers to all these questions. Perhaps once you answer them, whatever is holding you back will become clearer, and you can address solving that problem directly.

Jay Samit, a leading Hollywood media executive, author of the book *Disrupt You*, and one of my favorite TED speakers, draws the distinction between fear of failing and fear of failure.

Fear of failing, he explained, means giving up; whereas fear of failure is more about learning how it won't work. Failing is worse because it means you give up. Failure means you have found a way that something didn't work, and you'll continue to seek new ways.[88]

It seems we live in a time of extreme scrutiny and judgment. Just ask people how much they care about how many "likes" they get on social media. If someone writes a critical comment about us online, we can be devastated. Perhaps we see what other people do on their social media sites and think we can't compete with them, so why try? The reality is that most people post only the very best aspects of their lives online. If we try to compete with that, we're setting ourselves up for failure.

> Don't let the noise of others' opinions drown out your own inner voice.
>
> *Steve Jobs*

\* \* \*

One of my relatives is highly creative. When I asked him why he hadn't submitted his work for publication, he told me he didn't want to be successful. I didn't know how to react to that.

Assuming he would be successful, I asked him why that would be a problem for him. He said he didn't want to deal with having to talk with people about his success.

It sounded to me like he thought dealing with being successful would be a lot of work.

It seems that a lot of people talk themselves out of doing things because they're afraid it would involve too much work, or it might be too hard. How do they know if they don't try? Some people work so hard at not working, that if they spent that much time and energy working, they would have a lot more to show for it.

I once interviewed Lolly Daskal, a woman described as one of the most influential leadership coaches of our time. She's the author of *The Leadership Gap: What Gets Between You and Your Greatness*. During our interview,[89] she told me that leaders often fear people will discover they're not as smart as they appear to be or fear being exposed in some other way.

In one of her blogs,[90] she lists fears that many of us in the professional world have confronted at one time or another. They are fears we must overcome to move forward in our careers or our lives. The list includes fear of:

- Being criticized
- Being a failure
- Being a bad communicator
- Making hard decisions
- Not taking responsibility
- Not getting it done

They say curiosity killed the cat. Conversely, our fears may not kill our curiosity, but they can certainly wound it. Fear resulting from our curiosity is as common as curiosity itself. That said, how is it that some people can overcome that fear and go boldly into the realm of the unknown while others cannot? What enables them to say yes to the following questions when others hesitate? Should I:

- Explore this new opportunity?
- Invest in this stock or start-up?
- Quit my job to pursue my lifelong dream?
- Consider a new career?
- Throw my hat in the ring for this new position?

> Twenty years from now you will be more disappointed by the things you didn't do than by the ones you did do . . . Sail away from the safe harbor. Catch the trade winds in your sails. Explore. Dream. Discover.
>
> *Mark Twain*

One of my interviewees talked about continuing to be curious about what's on the other side. Yet, until we overcome any fear that's stopping us, it remains on the other side.

When I asked author, entrepreneur, and all-around maverick Yanik Silver about fear and curiosity, he told me, "Sometimes very traumatic things become alarm clocks, and other times they're quiet moments in which you hear a nagging little voice that says, 'There's something more.'

"If you're not feeling fully alive, if you're feeling a little depressed, if you're feeling frustrated, those are indications you're not truly following your path. Then it's up to you to do something about it. I believe following your heart is frequently scary, but it's never wrong. You can point to times when you said, 'I'm going to go do this.' Maybe you didn't even have a logical reason to do it, but in the end with an elevated viewpoint, you know it was the right move. Or it set up something else you never would have gotten to without going in that direction."

> Researchers at the University of Cincinnati found that 85% of what we worry about never happens. Also, 30% of the things feared happened in the past and cannot be changed, and 90% are insignificant issues.
>
> *Adam Kirk Smith, The Bravest You*[91]

### *Overcoming Our Fears*

So, how do we overcome our fears? You may be surprised at the answer. It's ironic, but according to scientists, the same curiosity that our fears can stymie is the antidote for overcoming our fears.

In short, they say, we need to be more childlike. As a child, researchers explain, curiosity is how we discover our world. It's how we learn. We're wide open to new experiences and unaware, and therefore unafraid, of the potential consequences. By the time we reach adulthood, we've experienced many of those consequences, so we've become more guarded, more conservative, in what we're willing to explore or not explore. So, for example, how could I break through my fear of exploring vegetables and consider cooking carrots in a new way?

According to scientists, I need to start by accepting the possibility that not all vegetables are the same, and perhaps those mushy carrots I ate early in my childhood weren't cooked in the best way. That single act of acceptance may be enough to encourage me to engage my curiosity about this whole mushy carrots thing. If I can get over my fear of reliving a negative experience from my past, scientists say, I'm more likely to be open to considering new and interesting recipes.

My thoughts immediately take me to the Bill Murray movie *What About Bob?* and its memorable line "Baby steps," or the Nike slogan, *Just do it!*

The aforementioned Jay Samit stated in his TED talk,[92] "Fear can either immobilize you or push you to challenge your perceived limits." Fear of letting his children down was his only motivation. For example, he admitted that he talked about a pretend company to make him appear more successful. He also put an ad in the paper for a fake job that would attract résumés so he could see what people offered. His stories are found in his book, *Disrupt You!: Master Personal Transformation, Seize Opportunity, and Thrive in the Era of Endless Innovation.*[93]

But what if your fear is more substantive? What if your fear is closer to being an impenetrable wall than a pane of glass?

Author Elizabeth Gilbert[94] inspired millions to choose a path of curiosity over that of fear. She delved into "how to overcome the fears and suffering that inevitably arise when we push at boundaries, embrace our curiosity and let go of fear."

Many of us talk ourselves into settling for how things have always been done because we fear the repercussions of making a change. Change is hard for most of us. If not change, sometimes choice. We fear other people's judgments if we make certain choices. They might make fun of us for trying something no one else has tried or tell us that it can't be done because they would be afraid to try it themselves.

What do we actually fear? Mostly, we fear change. However, embracing change can lead to some of the most innovative ideas. Warren Berger explained in *A More Beautiful Question* that there is "a direct connection between curious inquiry and many of today's most innovative entrepreneurs and designers. Design breakthroughs such as the Square credit card reader, Pandora internet radio, the Nest thermostat, and the business model for Airbnb all began with curious people wondering why a particular problem or human need existed and how it might best be addressed."

Brian Grazer is one of the most successful producers in Hollywood, with film credits that include *Splash*, *A Beautiful Mind*, and *Apollo 13*, along with TV hits such as '24,' 'Arrested Development,' 'Parenthood,' and the currently red-hot 'Empire.' So, what has helped Grazer climb to the top in one of the most competitive industries? Clearly, he has strong creative instincts and a great collaborative partner in Ron Howard, with whom Grazer co-founded Imagine Entertainment. But as Grazer sees it, one of his greatest assets—one that has fueled his success at every stage of his career—is his insatiable curiosity. 'Curiosity is what gives energy and insight to everything else I do,' Grazer wrote in his new book, *A Curious Mind: The Secret to a Bigger Life*.[95]

> When you take risks, you learn that
> there will be times when you succeed and
> there will be times when you fail, and
> both are equally important.
>
> *Ellen DeGeneres*

As Deborah Bowie stated so simply, "The opposite of fear is not bravery, but curiosity. When we know more, we fear less. That is true in every part of life—personal and professional."

Ellen Langer asked Harvard college students to give unprepared speeches to an audience. She wanted to see whether being open and curious could transform public speaking anxiety. How? By asking speakers to change their mindset about what constitutes a mistake.

Langer randomly assigned students to one of three conditions:

- the "mistakes are bad" condition, in which they were told not to make a mistake;

- the "forgiveness" condition, in which they were reassured that mistakes were fine and instructed to purposely make a mistake; and

- the "openness to novelty" condition, in which they were told to incorporate any mistakes they made into the speech itself and instructed to purposely make a mistake.

- Speakers in all three conditions gave a talk in front of a room full of people and were told they would be judged on how well they performed.

The results? Speakers in the "openness-to-novelty" condition judged themselves as more comfortable and rated their performance better than speakers in the other conditions. Moreover, the audience also judged the speakers in the "openness-to-novelty" condition as being more composed, effective, creative, and intelligent than speakers in the other two conditions.

In another experiment, a Japanese company wanted to train its employees to be more effective in doing business with their American counterparts. Japanese people can be innately shy and reluctant to assert themselves, especially in strange situations. Therefore, the CEO embarked on an interesting project to train his employees to overcome their shyness. Leaders of the firm were directed to go out into the streets of Tokyo during the busiest time of the day and sing their favorite song to unsuspecting crowds as if they were street performers. The employees were told that to overcome their fears, they must confront them head-on. Within months, the CEO began to see a more comfortable, more assertive workforce when interacting with foreign customers.

When asked why it's so important that we use curiosity to combat our fears, Richard Bandler, a leading author and self-help coach, said simply, "Because it beats the alternative! Curiosity is our means of survival. If we're not curious, we don't discover the world in which we live. We don't discover solutions to our problems. We don't improve. Like all organisms on planet earth, the fittest organisms are the ones that are able to adapt, and curiosity is the cornerstone of adaptation."[96]

In an interview with Brené Brown, who wrote the wonderful book *Braving the Wilderness: The Quest for True Belonging and the Courage to Stand Alone*[97] and others, she called fear a good thing, if we allow it. She described fear as "a sensation of vulnerability, which we tend to avoid." However, she advised, "We've got to be vulnerable. The three most powerful words I ever learned in my life were, 'I don't know.' Once I got comfortable with saying 'I don't know,' remarkable things happened. It's amazing how much you learn when you actually admit you don't know."

She added, "Courage starts with showing up—when we let ourselves be seen."[98]

Fear is the absolute opposite of curiosity. You don't look at things. You don't discover what works. You don't find out what's dangerous, and ultimately you don't progress or even survive.

> Constantly seek criticism. A well thought out
> critique of whatever you're doing is
> as valuable as gold.
>
> *Elon Musk*

\*   \*   \*

I once had the opportunity to interview CEO and co-founder of FiREapps, Wolfgang Koester.[99] His company helps corporations improve efficiencies, reduce costs, and reduce currency effects. He has over thirty years of extensive experience in currency markets and working with numerous global Fortune 1000 companies as well as government entities. He's steeped in such topics as interest before taxes and depreciation analysis, and he suggested we talk about the latest bitcoin issues.

I was simply not in the same league regarding financial matters. I knew that if I were to conduct the interview, I'd have to be a lot smarter about those issues. I had three options. I could:

1. not conduct the interview (fear of being exposed),

2. interview the man, feeling clearly uninformed about complex currency and tax matters (and be exposed), or

3. pursue my curiosity to know more about such things as blockchain and cryptocurrency.

Fortunately, my curiosity was the antidote to my fear. Behaviorists and business coaches alike encourage us not to shrink from the fear of the unknown or to allow our fears to shut down our curiosity. Instead, we're told to embrace our fears, to become curious about them, to examine them, to study their origins, and to learn what the unknown provokes in us and why.

> We cannot change what we are not aware of, and once we are aware, we cannot help but change.
>
> *Sheryl Sandberg*

As noted in previous chapters, highly successful leaders become comfortable exploring what makes them uncomfortable. This is the key to overcoming the first and mightiest of FATE.

As so many of my interviewees, leaders, and entrepreneurs have reminded me, to get closer to innovation means that we must get comfortable being uncomfortable.

# Chapter 13

# Curiosity and Assumptions

····················································

If I don't know I don't know, I think I know.
If I don't know I know, I think I don't know.

*R. D. Laing*

····················································

THINK ABOUT CHILDREN under five or six years old. Almost everything they see prompts a question. Their minds are blank slates, absorbing everything in their paths. If they get confused, they simply ask more questions. Without many prior experiences, young children have few assumptions from which to comprehend the world around them, only curiosity.

Then something happens.

While their childlike curiosity is theoretically a desirable and necessary trait, it can be an inconvenience or even an annoyance to those receiving the questions. (This can be true with adults as well.)

In research on this subject, teachers were given a list of common children's traits and asked to check those they found desirable in their students. Almost all checked curiosity. But when asked to list desirable traits from scratch, almost none mentioned curiosity. It seems that busy parents and overworked school teachers eventually seek relief from children's wondrous trait of seemingly endless questioning.

The problem comes when adults stop encouraging children to ask questions. Instead, we give them our own answers and simply tell them what to believe. The result? Eventually, they tend to stop asking questions and start assuming.

Given that scenario, by the time people are thirty or so, they've assumed their way to knowing all they need to know to survive in this world. They've soaked up knowledge and beliefs from parents, teachers, coaches, churches, college professors, and everyone else who has an opinion. While they may dismiss some of this mountain of data, what they accept they treat as fact, not to be questioned or disputed.

We are these grown-up children.

We accept that the moon landing was real (and not a hoax, as some websites suggest). We accept that hard work is the key to success and that exercise makes us healthier. Our knowledge base is rather well established. Facts are facts.

Or are they? While I do tend to agree with those assumptions, others I'm not so sure about. Quick: which of the following statements are true?

- Eating fatty food makes you fat.
- Gluten-free foods are healthier.
- Microwaving kills the nutrients in food.
- You'll lose a pound of fat for every 3,500 calories you burn.
- Spot training helps you burn fat in specific areas.

Would any of the above seem questionable and warrant further examination? While at one time the medical community believed all these statements to be true, all are now believed to be old wives' tales perpetuated by outdated information.

While we've learned a lot about health issues, it remains an evolving science, as do many aspects of our lives. Distinguishing truth from assumption is a never-ending process.

What about these assumptions?

- History books are accurate.

- We use only ten percent of our brains.

- If you heard it on the news, it must be true.

- If you want to know how a woman will look twenty years from now, look at her mother.

- Lightning never strikes twice in the same place.

These, too, are statements many people accept as true, but all have been debunked as myth.

Nevertheless, whatever our truths tend to be, factual or not, they give us our philosophical, physical, spiritual, and socioeconomic foundation. That foundation, however, is a combination of facts, near facts, and a whole lot of assumptions, the second of the FATE impediments to our curiosity.

> When we are open to new possibilities, we find them. Be open and skeptical of everything.
>
> *Todd Kashdan*

\* \* \*

Let face it, assumptions are necessary. They're also easy, convenient, and safe. They're how we get things done. Once we assume something to be true, we can move on with our life and plan accordingly.

The JFK assassination was complicated and full of mystery and uncertainty. The Warren Report on the assassination, by contrast, provided us with a neat set of assumptions (if we accepted them) that allowed us to move forward. The message was: Nothing to see here, folks. Keep moving.

If I go into business based on the assumption that I will generate $100,000 in revenue a month in my first year, and by month six I'm generating less than $3,000 a month, at what point do I question my assumptions? When do I become curious about why I'm not succeeding?

Assumptions are easy, but you see how they can bite us.

In contrast to these assumptions, curiosity is the perpetual fly in the ointment. Curiosity is the element that, instead of proceeding forward with an existing set of "truths," prompts us to stop the train.

Some people are constantly saying, "Hold on. Why are we doing it this way?" We can become annoyed with people who keep asking why because such inquiries can upset the apple cart. For example, executives at IBM became annoyed with H. Ross Perot's asking why services couldn't be provided more conveniently. He finally started his own consulting firm, EDS. Engineers became annoyed with Kenneth Olsen's asking why computers had to be the size of gymnasiums. He went on to create the mini-computer, which could sit on a desktop and was the precursor to the PC.

\*   \*   \*

Dr. Nick Morgan, a guest on my show and one of America's top communication theorists, said, "Curiosity can feel dangerous if it causes you to question the status quo. Practice curiosity by asking, 'Why do we do it this way? How could we do it differently? What's at stake if we do?'"

At what point do we inject our curiosity to challenge existing beliefs and assumptions? When they don't jive with our own beliefs and assumptions? When we don't get a satisfactory answer after asking why? How do we decide when it's best to "go along to get along" and when it's best to ask why?

Assumptions can feel safe and can be powerful

antidotes to curiosity. They provide a safe haven in which to move forward, even if they're only partially correct. Robert Stevenson, international public speaker and author of *How to Soar Like an Eagle in a World Full of Turkeys*,[100] told me of an interesting exercise he does with his audiences.

He tells people to put their hands over their watches to cover the faces. Then on the left side of the board, he writes I, II, III, and IV, and on the right side of the board, he writes I, II, III, and IIII. He proceeds to ask participants which set of numbers (right or left) would be the correct designations on a watch that has Roman numerals.

Most people, he said, pick the right side without question. But even though the Roman numeral IIII doesn't exist, it does appear on most watches using Roman numerals.

Interesting. I had to check this because I didn't believe it, but he got me, too. Many watches do use IIII, not IV. Because part of the information listed is correct, we assume that all the information is correct.

*     *     *

As we grow older, we become more comfortable with our surroundings and our truths. Our experiences shape our perceptions, and we make assumptions based on those experiences. Sometimes we do so doggedly, despite data to the contrary. When faced with an unfamiliar situation or a problem, our minds perceive it as a gap and hence a point of confusion or conflict. To resolve this discrepancy, our minds naturally tend to fill in the blanks with information obtained from what we know from our experiences. That's our frame of reference, our data base. Many times, we form our truth from those assumptions without even realizing it.

Jay Samit assumed that he had little chance in this world. Since childhood, he'd been told he wasn't smart enough to succeed due to his dyslexia. He carried this assumption with him as truth throughout his childhood and into his adult life until he learned that Steve Jobs, Ted Turner, Richard Branson, and about one third of all business owners were dyslexic.

We make decisions that shape our careers and our very lives based on assumptions that may or may not be true. If we fail, we often look to external reasons for those failures without considering our own assumptions.

James Pitaro, previously the chairman of Disney Consumer Products and Interactive Media, was named president of ESPN in 2016. ESPN is Disney's flagship sports and entertainment network. It had long served as the standard bearer for sports television, but the network had been lagging in ratings and revenues. The new president had his work cut out for him.

In his inaugural meeting with his new ESPN staff,[101] Pitaro drew a distinction between curiosity and assumptions, and he clarified which way he intended to take the network. He said, "If creativity is a process where new, original, and valuable ideas are developed, then operating on a foundation of assumption is likely to take us into the opposite direction of creativity."

H. R. "Bob" Haldeman, President Richard Nixon's chief of staff, famously said, "When it comes to the President, I have no curiosity, other than how to best execute his policy." Haldeman blindly assumed that Nixon's policies were the correct ones for the country. Those policies, some of which Haldeman knew to be contrary to truth and the law, led us to the Watergate scandal.

Gresham Brebach, managing partner for Digital Consulting, once said, "Computers are fast, accurate, and dumb. Humans are slow, inaccurate, and smart. Computers give us data and assumptions. Humans give us curiosity and creativity."

We sometimes assume that we won't like things for a variety of reasons. It may seem odd, or it may sound boring, or no one we know has experienced it. Maybe we played a game with a particular person and it wasn't fun, so we assumed that we didn't like the game. Then we tried playing it again with someone else, and it was lots of fun.

Do we resist something new based on assumptions, or are we willing to give it a try? From the shows we binge watch on TV to the mystery novels we read and reread and the foods we eat, what's familiar seems safer and more comfortable than what we haven't tried. Why disrupt things?

Author and former CEO G. Ross Kelly spoke of the differing responses he would get when challenging his employees. He described assumptions as the ultimate paradox of curiosity. "The more people discovered new knowledge," he said, "the more curious they became. They wanted to know more. In contrast, the more people assumed they already knew the answer, the less curious they became."

"Assumptions," he concluded, "generate complacency, whereas, curiosity discovers new thinking and innovation."

How do assumptions affect your curiosity? You'll have a chance to find out.

## Chapter 14

# Curiosity and Technology

· · · · · · · · · · · · · · · · · · · · · · · · · · · · · · · · · · ·

With Google I'm starting to burn out on knowing the answer to everything. People in the year 2020 are going to be nostalgic for the sensation of feeling clueless.

*Douglas Copeland*

· · · · · · · · · · · · · · · · · · · · · · · · · · · · · · · · · · ·

D OES TECHNOLOGY INHIBIT or enhance our curiosity?

When I have asked myself or others that question, the answers I got depended on whether I asked people who develop technology or people who consume technology.

The developers of technology said that they find their curiosity enhanced by the infinite possibilities that technology offers. Recall, for example, the evolution of computers over the past fifty years. In the 1960s, computing technology was housed in and mostly developed through large mainframe computers the size of a living room. As the state of the art evolved into the 1970s, the computing power of those large mainframes was condensed into desktop mini-computers a hundredth the size and ten times as powerful. Mini-computers evolved into laptops, which offered the same or more computing power in smaller, more convenient packaging. From laptops, we progressed to tablets and mobile phones, and today we have what's referred to as wearable technology and nanotechnology.

Imagine the curiosity that resulted in the integrated circuit. Imagine Steve Jobs' curiosity around the subject of calligraphy and his application of that curiosity to the creation of unusual computer fonts. That kind of curiosity has continued to drive the question: how do we make computing technology more accessible, faster, more powerful, more aesthetically pleasing, more secure, and more able to solve problems?

Can we even imagine how curious technologists, entrepreneurs, engineers, and bioscientists must be as they pursue the next version of a smartphone, smart kitchen, self-driving cars, or cures for diseases? Whatever the next generation of innovations may be, people will achieve it by combining the infinite wonders of technology with equally infinite doses of curiosity.

When asked how many versions of the iPod there would be, Jobs once responded, "As long as we're curious, there's no telling."

* * *

Despite the spurring of their own curiosity by technology, some creators fear that for the rest of us, the mere consumers and beneficiaries, all the innovations may be lessening our curiosity.

Scott Hanselman, a Microsoft-based web technologist and teacher of computer technologies, views the world in binary terms of those who are curious and those who are not. Possibly deriving from his parents' lessons in his childhood of a fixed mindset versus a growth mindset, he believes that the more technology advances, the more it seems like magic. This magic eliminates curiosity about how it works.

He asks in a video presentation,[102] "Is twenty-first-century technology making it too easy? Are iPhones so magical sitting atop the last millennium of technology that it's not worth teaching, or even wondering, how it all fits together?" He clearly defines himself as one who is curious. "I took apart my toaster, my remote control, and a clock-radio telephone before I was ten. Didn't you?

"What's the difference between the people who take toasters apart and the folks who just want toast? At what point do kids or young adults stop asking, 'How does it work?' Perhaps curiosity is an innate thing; perhaps it's taught and encouraged, but likely it's a little of both.

"I hope you're stretching yourself and others to ask more questions and explore the how and why of the world around you."

Kishau Rogers is a senior technologist and CEO of the Websmith Group, a corporation that helps organizations take new technologies from conception to commercialization. She suggests that rather than teach children how to code, we should teach them how to think about systems.

"If we simply accept technologies as somehow magically providing us the answers, we have no reason to be curious about how those answers were conceived." We don't need to know the intricacies, she suggests, but at least we should understand the basics of how we got there.

Naomi Karten leverages her background in both psychology and technology to help organizations improve customer satisfaction and strengthen teamwork. In a speech, she explained, "It's the ease of access that seems to be of greatest concern. Kids today can pull up Wikipedia and find page after page of data. But are they learning anything? And the situation isn't any better for us adults. Consider the news. Instead of reading it daily via print, we can now get the news all day long from our phones, tablets, laptops, and televisions. We have easy access, but are we any more or any better informed?

"There's an understandable concern that the instant gratification we derive from technology is making us less likely to be curious about increasingly difficult problems. By filling our brains with easy answers, we become less likely to go after complex problems."

Consumers of technology seem to have a slightly different view.

Fifty years ago, if we were to search for the population of Duluth, Minnesota, we would resort to *Encyclopedia Britannica,* which would most likely be out of date. We would then cross-reference our information with three other sources to verify the encyclopedia's accuracy. After researching the question for thirty to forty-five minutes, we would have our answer, knowing it still may not be quite accurate or complete.

Today, we have Siri or Alexa or other comparable technologies that will find our answer in less time than it took me to type this sentence.

By the way, Siri told me that as of 2010, the population of Duluth, Minnesota was 86,265, and I didn't have to type this sentence. I dictated it through the wonders of voice activation.

Does that mean that as a consumer of these marvels of technology, a user rather than a developer, I'm any less curious than the developers of the iPad, or Siri, or smart cars? Am I somehow less curious than the bioengineer who tirelessly pursues the cure for Alzheimer's?

Nicholas Carr, author of the book *The Shallows: What the Internet Is Doing to Our Brains,* described the dilemma technology seems to create. "On the one hand, I can now do in minutes that which once required days. On the other hand, I feel I'm not thinking the way I used to."

He continued, "I feel it most strongly when reading. Immersing myself in a book or a lengthy article used to be easy. My mind would get caught up in the narrative or the turns of the argument, and I'd spend hours strolling through long stretches of prose. That's rarely the case anymore. Now my concentration often starts to drift after two or three pages. I get fidgety, lose the thread, and begin looking for something else to do."[103]

That's how technology can affect our concentration. Then there's the issue of retention.

Technology may help us to find information more quickly and efficiently, but do we retain that information the way we used to? Many behaviorists, supported by research, argue that the longer the time and greater the effort required to obtain information, the better we retain that information.

So, are we any smarter?

If we want to continue to develop our ability to improve what technology can do for us, we need to open our minds and develop our sense of curiosity.

\*   \*   \*

Jason Kintzler, CEO and founder of Pitchengine, said on my show that you can create disruptive technology from the most unlikely places. For example, a disruptive technology is when something like Uber unsettles the traditional transportation industry or how Netflix upset the video industry.

Some technologists are working to incorporate a form of curiosity right into technology. For example, developers at the University of California at Berkeley are attempting to create a curiosity-based video game. The team developed an intrinsic curiosity model to make their learning algorithm work even without a strong feedback or reward mechanism. An AI software program employs curiosity-based attributes and logic. The model in the video game controls a virtual agent that seeks to maximize its understanding of its environment and act based on its understanding of that environment.

Efforts such as these are emerging as new directions in the development of AI, recognizing the concern that technology can potentially have a limiting effect on our curiosity.

Astrophysicist Mario Livio presented another slant on the issue. He wrote a book on curiosity simply titled *Why?* There, he reminded us that curiosity is a given, an intrinsic part of our nature. Perceptual curiosity, as defined, is a natural element of who we are, and it can be enhanced by technology.

As he explained, "There are some people who have the feeling that because we have information literally at our fingertips, maybe we're becoming less curious. But that's not true. There are two things to remember. One is that when we do scientific research, we try to find answers to questions where we don't know the answers yet. Therefore, you cannot find those answers on the internet or Wikipedia.

"The other thing the internet allows us to do is to satisfy what has been dubbed specific curiosity, namely you want to know a very particular detail. Who wrote this or that book? What was the name of the actor in that film? The digital age allows you to find the answer very quickly. That's actually good because you don't want to spend all your time trying to answer a question like that."[104]

According to Kintzler, technology doesn't make us less curious; rather, it makes us more efficient in our search for answers to questions driven by our curiosity.

\* \* \*

Whether technology inhibits or enhances our curiosity, scientists say that we must find new ways to learn in light of the fact that technology is able to provide information so readily.

The Association for Educational Communications and Technology examined that issue. Arnone, Small, Chauncey, and McKenna concluded that while our curiosity, interest, and engagement in the pursuit of learning has remained essentially the same, how we research and engage information-seeking tasks has significantly changed. They stated, "We need to create new and innovative ways to study and apply curiosity, in light of the availability of pervasive technologies."[105]

The company Survey Monkey provides an excellent illustration of the balance between technology and curiosity. This online survey company has grown to be a multimillion-dollar enterprise using its technology to solicit and analyze data, all based on the theme of curiosity.

"Curiosity is one of the things that CEOs need to have in their companies, and also one of the attributes they look for in leaders," said Senior Vice President of Marketing Communications Bennett Porter. "And that's really the essence of what people told us they use Survey Monkey for: not to make a decision, but to have enough data to know they were headed in the right direction."[106]

As CEO Zander Lurie stated, "Not being sufficiently curious is bad for business, especially when a company faces unexpected problems. Often someone in management or a team in management or a CEO didn't ask the right questions and listen and learn. So we see this big opportunity to help companies turn those voices into actual data."

Notice how the name "Survey Monkey" is even grounded in the curiosity theme; it's based on the idea that monkeys are innately curious about the world around them. The company's marketing also features catchphrases such as "Power to the curious."

*   *   *

The chasm between developers of technology and consumers of technology appears to be narrowing. A general consensus was summarized by Ashok Shah, former vice president of services at Compaq Computer and Lucent Technologies and author of *Emergence of the "Me" Enterprise: A Blueprint for Leadership in the 21st Century*. He wrote, "Whichever side of the fence you are on, the more we can bring curiosity and technology together in an integrated fashion, the smarter we will be."[107]

## Chapter 15

# Curiosity and the Environment

. . . . . . . . . . . . . . . . . . . . . . . . . . . . . . . . . . . . . . . . . . . . .

[In school] I encountered authority of a different
kind than I had ever encountered before, and
I did not like it . . . . They came close to really
beating any curiosity out of me.

*Steve Jobs*

. . . . . . . . . . . . . . . . . . . . . . . . . . . . . . . . . . . . . . . . . . . . .

W HEN CONSIDERING CURIOSITY, our environment includes the hopes, dreams, guidance, expectations, opinions, and instructions given to us throughout our lives. All are powerful in shaping who we are and who we become. Our indoctrination begins with our parents and continues with our teachers, coaches, ministers, college professors, politicians, bosses, colleagues, next-door neighbors, and all the other influential figures in our lives. Their messages, positive or negative, shape our own beliefs, attitudes, and behaviors. They also shape our curiosity.

We're either being encouraged or discouraged in our curiosity. We're being influenced as to what we should be curious about, as well as what to accept as givens.

This shaping begins with our parents.

As children, we want to know everything! From, why do birds have feathers on their faces, to how are horses different from mules, our endless questions are all over the map. Every response to those questions either encourages or suppresses our curiosity.

The nonstop questions of a four-year-old can take their toll on an overworked, exasperated parent. Unfortunately, "just because" isn't an answer that engenders a child's curiosity.

As astronomer and author Neil deGrasse Tyson put it, "Kids are born scientists. They are curious about everything around them. And a parent can either respond 'Let's find out' or 'Stop asking so many questions!'"[108]

Input continues with our teachers and education system.

Researchers and behavioral scientists have long decried that our education system places more emphasis on maintaining order and teaching answers than it does encouraging questions or curiosity. Teachers are given curricula and lesson plans to administer. Standardized tests measure students' proficiency as well as teachers' effectiveness. Rarely, if ever, are teachers measured on how much curiosity they instilled in their students.

Doug Bergum is an American entrepreneur, philanthropist, and politician serving as the thirty-third and current governor of North Dakota. In a TED talk,[109] he spoke at length about the environmental pressures from parents, teachers, religious leaders, and others to conform to conventional wisdom.

He then described discoveries such as those resulting from Columbus's voyage to the New World and innovations such as those by the Wright Brothers, Thomas Edison, and others. These discoveries and innovations, he said, required two critical ingredients: perseverance and courageous curiosity.

He spoke of the many failures each of these pioneers endured before realizing their success. He cited their determination to persevere and their courageous curiosity in an environment filled with doubt, ridicule, and in some cases, physical harm. Our environment, he claimed, is dominated by answers and devoid of questions. "It's like gravity," he added. "It holds us down, and it's only by perseverance and courageous curiosity that we are able to defy that gravitational pull."

He concluded his remarks by revealing that when he dropped off his kids at school each morning, instead of saying, "Have a nice day," he'd tell them, "Ask great questions today."

Developmental psychologists Barbara Tizard and Martin Hughes conducted research and found that while kindergarten-age children asked an average of twenty-seven questions an hour at home, that number plummeted to only about three when they were at school. Some of this drop-off, the authors concluded, is unavoidable. Kids at school don't have the opportunity to ask questions endlessly as they might at home. However, this could be off-set somewhat if the school environment would encourage children to be more curious.

Many are convinced that curiosity is drastically underappreciated in our educational institutions. Susan Engel, author of *The Hungry Mind*, said that amidst the country's standardized testing mania, schools are missing what most matters about learning, the desire to learn in the first place. From her studies, teachers rarely encourage curiosity in the classroom, even though that's the one factor that can most influence learning.[110]

Leslie Crawford, senior editor at Great Schools, described behaviors of parents and teachers that can have a subtle but lasting effect on a child's curiosity. She mentioned behaviors such as overreacting to a child's mess, choosing what a child should study, over-scheduling a child's time, being overly concerned with safety, and having all the answers. Each of these behaviors can suppress natural curiosity in children.

The author asserted that the messy but creative art of slime-making, so popular among children, can engender the scientists, engineers, and inventors of the future. She admonished, let them make messes!

Beneficial environmental influences such as the STEM (science, technology, engineering, and mathematics) Program and the Curiosity Cube are attempting to stimulate and sustain the innate curiosity of children. The program encourages a curriculum in schools to improve competitiveness in the science and technology fields. The Curiosity Cube is a renovated shipping container turned into a traveling learning laboratory. Sponsored by the Millipore organization, the Curiosity Cube encourages students to explore subjects in the areas of science, technology, and engineering.

*   *   *

In conclusion, the shaping and coaching process of our environment continues from our childhoods well into our adult lives and, in reality, is never-ending. From our parents, teachers, and pastors to our bosses and even media advertising, the messaging is nonstop. It's all in pursuit of our mindshare and either encourages or represses our curiosity. In a world dominated by policies, procedures, rules, and guidelines, traits such as creativity and innovation are the domain of the curious and the courageous.

Thus, the influences of our environment along with the elements of FATE most affect our level of curiosity.

For us as individuals and for the companies that employ us, to what degree do FATE factors control our curiosity? In turn, to what extent does this control obstruct our creativity, innovation, and productivity? Most important, to what extent can those barriers be torn down, thereby unleashing the creativity, innovation, and productivity within us and within our companies?

Those questions are for us to answer with the help of the Curiosity Code Index that accompanies this book. A preview of the Code is presented in Chapter 17.

# PART III

# *Doing Something about It*

# Chapter 16

# Measuring Curiosity

. . . . . . . . . . . . . . . . . . . . . . . . . . . . . . . . . . . . . . . . . . . .

*If you can't measure it, it doesn't exist.*

*Anonymous*

. . . . . . . . . . . . . . . . . . . . . . . . . . . . . . . . . . . . . . . . . . . .

I F YOU SUBSCRIBE to the axiom that for something to exist it must be measurable (which I do), we have our work cut out for us. Multiple studies have been conducted about curiosity, and numerous tools help us measure its various aspects.

According to behavioral scientists, we have intellectual curiosity, trait curiosity, state curiosity, epistemic curiosity, and perceptual curiosity. Some of us even have the curiosity of chimpanzees under stress. Assessment instruments exist to measure each of these, ranging from simple questionnaires to double-blind assessments. For example, how would you respond to the following?

I get bored easily. Y/N?

I don't care how it works as long as it works. Y/N?

I love the excitement of the unknown. Y/N?

I like repetition. Y/N?

I prefer word searches to riddles. Y/N?

I'll try anything once to see what it's like. Y/N?

I enjoy trying new approaches. Y/N?

If you want to measure your curiosity in a more elaborate fashion, try the Kashdan Scale, the Melbourne

Curiosity Inventory, or the California Critical Thinking Disposition Inventory (CCTDI). Measurements are available for virtually every type of curiosity we may have.

However, that is not the purpose of the Curiosity Code Index.

My goal was not to create another assessment instrument to measure one's level of curiosity, but to assess what inhibits our curiosity. Why does the natural, childlike curiosity we are born with wane as we age? We know that fear, assumptions, technology, and the environment (FATE) are major factors that influence our curiosity, but which ones affect it a lot and which ones only a little bit, if at all? And by how much?

To fully unleash the leadership and innovation that reside within each of us and within our workforce, we need to know more about these inhibitors. Thus, the two basic hypotheses of this book and the Curiosity Code Index are that:

1. Curiosity is integral to all we do in life, especially if we do it well. From innovation to creativity, motivation and leadership to leading a meaningful life, curiosity is a critical difference maker that distinguishes between truly living life and merely existing.

2. Somewhere along that path of life, our curiosity can wane, and we may even go so far as

to fall into a rut. Some say this is due to the aging process itself. (It isn't.) Some say our ability to learn begins to wane naturally as we age. (It doesn't.) So, what is it that inhibits our curiosity, and how do we get it back?

After years of research and literally thousands of interviews, I have found so many examples that defy the stereotypical assumption that age is the reason we lose our curiosity. It seems that people who are highly successful demonstrate higher levels of curiosity than those who are less successful, no matter what their endeavor or age.

The evidence is clear that people such as Elon Musk, Steve Forbes, Deepak Chopra, and Tony Robbins have taken their curiosity to new heights. Others appear to be more sporadic, less enthused, less curious. So, if it's not age, and if it's not physical or mental deterioration, then what is it?

That's what I endeavored to find out.

The answer, it appeared, was not a function of natural deterioration, but of choice.

I learned that our curiosity remains with us through-out our lives. But like a pair of shoes, we choose if and when to employ it. Better yet, we allow choices to be made for us. I learned that the inhibitors to our curiosity are not as much physical or mental as they are societal.

All of this brought me to the central question: what

are those societal forces that lead us to the choice to be curious or incurious? That pursuit ultimately revealed the big four categories of FATE.

After my research, my interviews, and my discussions with CEOs, entrepreneurs, and business leaders, I had confirmed my conclusions, but they had yet to be proven. They had to be tested. And more important, I had to create a way to measure them.

Earlier, I had become certified to give multiple assessments such as the EQ-i or the MBTI. However, I had never considered creating a valid assessment instrument on my own. And I'm not talking about the kind that determines the best barbeque sauce or your favorite Tom Hanks movie. I'm talking about an assessment that must be scientifically validated and pass muster with theorists, academics, and behavioral scientists.

I couldn't simply assert that some combination of our fears and assumptions, technology, and our environment are the major factors influencing our curiosity. Which is most prevalent? Is it fear? Is it our environment? Is it some combination of the four? Is it all the above? I had to test and validate my assumptions. After all, weren't assumptions part of the problem? I needed to become more curious.

In the next chapter I present to you a preview of the companion item to this book, the Curiosity Code Index.

*Chapter 17*

# The Curiosity Code Index

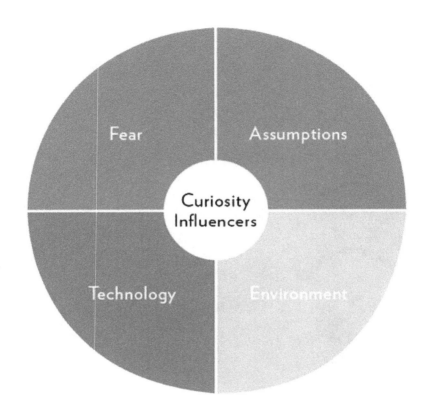

### The Curiosity Code Index

The Curiosity Code Index (CCI) is designed to help you gain insights into the factors that inhibit your curiosity and to what degree. Only then can you take meaningful steps to overcome those forces and optimize the creativity, motivation, and productivity that allow you to learn, lead, and live most successfully.

The CCI is designed to be used by individuals,

companies, and other organizations. The ideal scenario is to train and certify the designees of CEOs, division managers, human resource professionals, and the like to guide their employees through the assessment process.

Then corporations and businesses can formulate a company-wide initiative and strategy to unleash their collective innovation, levels of engagement, and leadership potential.

You will find the Curiosity Code Index to be brief and easy to complete. You might even regard the questions as rather simplistic. However, quite the opposite is true.

Be it fear, assumptions, technology, environment, or a combination, all of us experience factors that affect our curiosity, our interest in exploring, and our creativity. While the questions are seemingly simple and straightforward, each will require thought and can reveal interesting findings.

Your answers will clearly indicate which combination of those factors is the biggest impediment to your curiosity. More important, you'll learn what you can do about those answers to better your life.

CEOs, business leaders, and entrepreneurs alike say that if they could re-inject their employees with a dose of childlike curiosity, the innovativeness, competitiveness, and success of their businesses would immeasurably improve.

That's exactly what I hope the CCI can do for you and your company.

Following is a summary of the Curiosity Code Index assessment instrument and how it explores your curiosity with the four stated domains of fear, assumptions, technology, and environment (FATE).

### Curiosity Code Index—Fear

The first factor in the CCI is Fear. The assessment explores to what extent you tend to avoid experimenting with new things based on fear of the potential outcome.

Do you hesitate because you don't want to look foolish? Are you concerned that your interests aren't in line with what others deem worthy? Or do you relish the excitement of the unknown?

Would you consider yourself to be a risk taker or risk averse? The questionnaire explores how fearful you may be of the risks involved in a potential outcome. That fear blocks your curiosity and desire to explore potential opportunities or new situations.

Be it a fear of failure, fear of the potential outcome, or fear of how others may view us, the Fear quadrant in the CCI explores them all to determine to what extent fear inhibits your curiosity.

### Curiosity Code Index—Assumptions

The CCI examines assumptions to assess to what degree preconceived ideas influence your curiosity. Ideas about what works, what doesn't work, how things work, and how they could work better all affect your curiosity. But do those ideas inhibit your curiosity, and if so, to what extent?

Do you have the self-confidence to make important decisions because you assume you know the outcome? Or do you assume a negative result from trying something new because of a bad experience with something similar in the past?

Do you tend to tell yourself that something is boring, uninteresting, or a waste of time simply because that's what you've been led to believe based on limited exposure? Or do you try it anyway?

### *Curiosity Code Index—Technology*

While technology has opened a world of opportunities, it has also created reliance on it and sometimes fear of it. Do you avoid learning how to operate technology or look at it as an impediment to learning? Or do you welcome the opportunity to learn it for the convenience it provides?

Are you so dependent on social media that you base many of your decisions and choices on what your friends do? Or are you so turned off by social media that you avoid being around people who embrace it?

The internet offers a world of knowledge, but it can be challenging to keep up with all the advances. Do you want to keep up with how all the latest internet innovations work, or would you prefer someone explain them to you?

Having technological skills can be important for career success. Do you hold on to old ways of doing things because they worked well in the past, or do you enjoy embracing changes in technology with proactive preparation?

### Curiosity Code Index—Environment

Some of us were fortunate to have parents, teachers, and other adults who allowed us, even encouraged us, to explore. Others may have been shackled by parental and societal beliefs and restrictions.

How did your upbringing and education influence your current modus operandi?

Do you tend to go along with what is expected of you from family, friends, or teachers instead of going in the direction you would naturally head?

Do you tend to avoid trying new things or meeting new people, or do you enjoy that kind of stimulation?

Do you naturally think outside the box unless you're not rewarded for that thinking or are told not to be difficult? Or do you ignore the opinions of others and do your own thing?

The CCI helps you assess the degree to which your environment has impeded or enhanced your curiosity and creativity.

\*   \*   \*

What if every CEO, division director, business owner, or HR director had their workforce complete this questionnaire? What if afterwards they conducted a review of their findings and their discoveries about themselves?

What if then, in a workshop or brainstorming setting, they created a series of action plans to overcome the barriers they uncovered? And what if they had a systematic way to encourage the fulfillment of those action plans and followed up accordingly?

What if this process resulted in increased productivity, increased levels of engagement, and increased levels of motivation and innovation?

Finally, what if all that translated into an entire workforce that was more engaged and more focused than ever, and a company that was more competitive, more productive, and more successful than most?

Yes, it's possible.

\*   \*   \*

The Curiosity Code Index (CCI) is designed for individuals or groups in a corporate or company setting. Either way, the assessment is administered by a trained, certified administrator, and the results are confidential.

Further details on how the CCI assessment is administered and tabulated, as well as how to become trained and certified to administer the CCI, are provided in the Appendix.

# *Conclusion*

. . . . . . . . . . . . . . . . . . . . . . . . . . . . . . . . . . . . . . . . . . . . . . . .

I am neither especially clever nor especially
gifted. I am only very, very curious.

*Albert Einstein*

. . . . . . . . . . . . . . . . . . . . . . . . . . . . . . . . . . . . . . . . . . . . . . . .

WHEN I BECAME intrigued with the subject of curiosity and began writing this book, I was largely driven by my own curiosity to better understand its effect on our lives. I wanted to know what, if any, correlation existed between curiosity and intelligence and curiosity and motivation. In general, I wanted to understand the effects of curiosity on our performance as human beings.

Further, I wanted to know how curiosity interacts with other emotional and behavioral drivers. My goal was not only to better understand the subject of curiosity, but also to learn more about how we apply it to become better leaders and better human beings.

The more I dug into the topic, however, every answer I uncovered seemed to yield a new and different question. Is curiosity a conscious action? Or is it an intrinsic, unconscious behavior?

Do we have the freedom of choice to determine our curiosity? Are those who are highly motivated first curious about the subject, then motivated? Or is it the other way around? If I'm motivated, am I therefore curious? Or does it go both ways? The topic was far more complex and confusing than I had originally anticipated.

As I studied, I was taken back to the book by the famed psychiatrist R. D. Laing, *Knots*.[111] He stated:

> I was beginning to feel like that around the subject of curiosity and motivation. One simple definition of curiosity is "a strong desire to know or learn something." Simple enough, right? But the more I studied, the more I discovered various *types* of curiosity.

I simply wanted to learn how to use curiosity to become a better leader. I wasn't prepared to be taken down the many rabbit holes of state curiosity, trait curiosity, curiosity and motivation, emotional curiosity, the curiosity of fear, or the many other dimensions of the subject.

Then, it gradually made sense.

- Curiosity is the interest to learn more about a subject; motivation is the desire to do something with that knowledge.
- Discovering the unfamiliar within the familiar . . .
- Bringing a beginner's mind to old problems . . .
- I wonder if the burner will be hot if I touch it now . . .

Although the topic and its complexities have intrigued business leaders and behavioral scientists for decades, it can be distilled to a childlike simplicity. It's the ultimate paradox of human behavior.

It begins with survival. We, like all other animals, are naturally curious, much the way we naturally pursue food and sex. Curiosity may vary from individual to individual, as we are all born with some degree of trait curiosity. It's a foundational element of our existence.

From there, the rest is up to us. We can develop it or not.

Whether we're mildly curious, passionately curious, emotionally curious, or fearful of curiosity is ultimately a matter of choice.

We are born with a strong Curiosity Quotient. But as we age and enter the travails of living, that CQ can ebb. Some people retain that childlike curiosity; many do not.

Knowing that, my focus shifted. I concluded that the analysis and measure of curiosity had been studied and researched for decades by scientists and researchers who were far more learned than I.

My interest moved to this set of questions:

- If what is intrinsic to us all begins to wane as we age, and that deterioration cannot be attributed to the aging process itself, then why does it wane?

- What are the forces that cause our curiosity to ebb?

- Can those forces be overcome?

- Can we regain that natural ability to be curious?

Through my research and interviews, the answers to the question of what forces cause deterioration of our curiosity fell into the categories I refer to as FATE: fear, assumptions, technology, and environment.

As reflected throughout this book, I quizzed my radio guests as well as my friends, family members, and colleagues on these topics. Unknowingly, they became my guinea pigs and early subjects to test my theories. To them, I became a broken record. To them, I became annoyingly predictable in my questions and conversations. *Why do people lose their curiosity?* This became my obsession.

Now that we know and appreciate the significance of curiosity, the question arises of how to apply that knowledge. We know the importance of curiosity as it relates to employee engagement, emotional intelligence, productivity, innovation, critical thinking, and so on. But how do we convert that knowledge into tangible gains—both for individuals and for corporations?

*Cracking the Curiosity Code* is not intended to stand alone as an intellectual exercise to better understand curiosity. Rather, it's bundled with the actionable

Curiosity Code Index and I-Workshops. They provide individuals and corporations with a serious tool and process to achieve greater gains in employee engagement, innovation, and productivity.

I hope you will find all three components to be highly valuable.

# About the Author

D R. DIANE HAMILTON is President and Founder of Tonerra, a global coaching and consulting firm. She is also a nationally syndicated radio host, speaker, and educator. Through her work as the MBA Program Chair at the Forbes School of Business and several other universities, she has taught more than a thousand business courses. She has earned a PhD in Business Management and is a certified Myers-Briggs MBTI and Emotional Intelligence EQ-i instructor.

Dr. Hamilton has advised and inspired Fortune 500 executives and entrepreneurs to increase engagement, improve productivity, and reduce conflict. She has authored multiple books, including a text on personality assessments that was required reading at a university in Arizona.

# *Acknowledgments*

THIS HAS BEEN an extremely rewarding and challenging process that has involved many incredible people.

First and foremost, I would like to thank G. Ross Kelly, who has inspired me to strive to be a better writer. He has my undying gratitude, for without him this book would not have been possible.

Many people I have interviewed have been instrumental to the content in this book. I would like to thank everyone whom I have interviewed, with special recognition to Steve Forbes, Keith Krach, Dion Graham, Jay Samit, Jeffrey Hayzlett, Ken Fisher, Verne Harnish, Robin Farmanfarmaian, Craig Newmark, Guy Winch, Naveen Jain, Ford Saeks, Lolly Daskal, Kevin Sheridan, Leonard Kim, Tanner Gers, Michelle Tillis Lederman, Roya Mahboob, Mitch Russo, Ron Shaich, Kare Anderson, Kevin Kruse, Warren Berger, Matt Abrahams, Jason Kintzler, Douglas Conant, Jeff Hoffman,

Liz Wiseman, Dr. Gilda Carle, Jason Ma, Professor M. S. Rao, Kevin Surace, Tom Kolditz, Dr. Katie Thiry, Dr. Maja Zelehic, Tony Alessandra, Marshall Goldsmith, Sally Helgesen, Dave Ulrich, Erik Weihenmayer, Kevin Cashman, Dr. Bob Nelson, Dr. Henry Cloud, Larry Robertson, Vanessa Maynard, Emily Verstege, Doyle Buehler, Michael Hvisdos, Gregory Mirzayantz, Mike Federle, Mark Sanborn, Scott DuPont, Joe Calloway, Adam Markel, Michael Bungay Stanier, Garry Ridge, Simon T. Bailey, Mark Divine, Yanik Silver, Wolfgang Koester, Dr. Nick Morgan, Robert Stevenson, and my family.

# *Appendix*

THE APPENDIX PROVIDES additional information on how the Curiosity Code Index is administered and what you can do with your results.

It is structured into two categories of information:

- *For Individuals*, who choose to take the CCI Assessment on their own; and,

- *For Groups*, including those that take the CCI Assessment as part of a Corporate or Company initiative.

### *For Individuals*

We are reminded by behavioral scientists and business leaders alike that self-awareness is essential to success in any endeavor. If you are not aware of what motivates you and what holds you back, you are significantly limited in what you can accomplish for yourself and your company. That is the purpose of the Curiosity Code Index (CCI).

The CCI can be taken online by anyone interested in learning their level of Curiosity Quotient (CQ) by going to curiositycode.com.

Just as with other online assessment instruments, the CCI can be taken in less than twenty minutes, and the results will be immediate. It is helpful to have a trained professional review the results, but it is not required.

Once you have received your results, recommended actions will be provided in each of the categories of Fear, Assumptions, Technology, and Environment. Descriptions of each follow.

## *Fear*

As you begin to better understand how fear affects your curiosity, you will learn how to address issues such as how to deal with perceptions of failure, embarrassment, and loss of control. There could be specific issues like competition, pressure, rejection, and expectations. Depending on your results, you will receive input regarding how to create an action plan for each of the issues. This action plan includes things like goals, timeframes, potential outcomes, threats, and support system options.

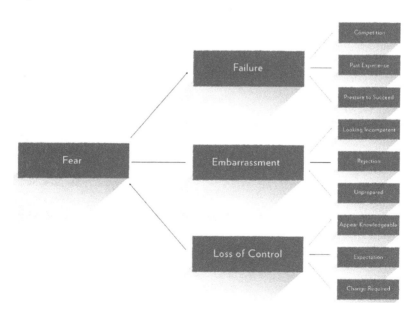

### Assumptions

As you learn more about how assumptions affect your curiosity, you will discover the subtle, sometimes undetectable, factors that inhibit your willingness to explore or be curious. From the issues or topics that you disliked as a child, to the areas you believed to be already sufficiently explored, you will discover the subtlety and significance of those assumptions that curtailed or blocked your curiosity.

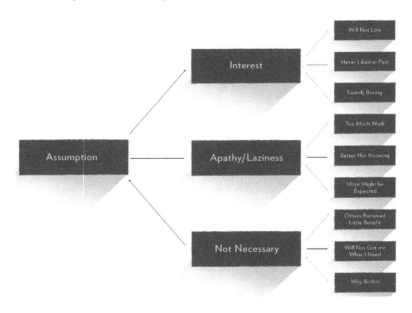

*Technology*

The third factor the CCI will assess is how technology influences your curiosity. You may believe that Siri or Alexa can answer questions regarding any curiosity you may have, or you may be overwhelmed by the onslaught of technology. Or you may resist the inevitable changes that accompany new technologies. Whatever it is, and to whatever extent, the CCI will help you better understand.

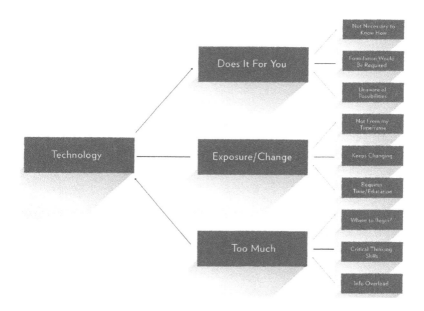

### *Environment*

The fourth and final factor assessed by the CCI is the degree to which your parents, your college professors, your pastor, and all the other influential people in your life influence and potentially inhibit your curiosity. It may be your culture; it may be your boss.

Whatever and to what extent, the CCI assesses the impact of your environment as it relates to your curiosity.

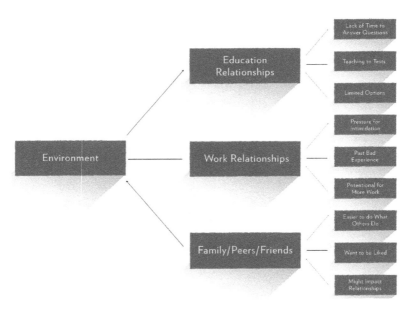

In less time than it takes to change the settings of an iPhone, an individual can take the Curiosity Code Index assessment and receive personal results with a series of suggested actions to improve their curiosity.

As suggested, trained and certified professionals can assist individuals with their assessment results or recommended actions.

After you take the CCI as an individual and conclude the instrument to be valuable for your group or corporation, you'll find information on the Curiosity Code website (curiositycode.com) for group or corporate initiatives.

Group initiatives, which are discussed in the following section, have proven to improve employee engagement, innovation, and productivity, among other benefits.

### *For Groups or Organizations:*

Group or corporate initiatives in which group members or employees take the CCI as a team have proven to significantly improve:

- *Employee engagement*
- *Motivation*
- *Creativity*
- *Innovation*
- *Productivity*

Organizational initiatives related to the Curiosity Code Index encompass a series of actions that closely monitor the results and ensuing actions embedded in what is referred to as an I-Plan (Innovation Plan).

The I-Plan is managed by an outside consultant or an in-house designee who is trained and certified to administer the instrument while overseeing the corporate initiative.

What follows is a brief overview of the elements of the I-Plan and its outputs.

### The I-Plan

Combined with this book, *Cracking the Curiosity Code*, and the assessment Curiosity Code Index, the I-Plan offers a structured series of workshops and actions to improve a company's or division's innovation and productivity.

The I-Plan contains the following:

- The book, *Cracking the Curiosity Code*
- The assessment instrument, the Curiosity Code Index
- The I-Workshop series
- The participant recommendations
- The Corporate Action Plan

The series of products and events is concluded by a specific series of actions embedded in the Corporate Action Plan. It also includes follow-up activities to monitor and ensure that the actions of those recommended steps will improve motivation, innovation, productivity, and employee engagement.

The intended objective of any I-Plan is a collection of outcomes that can be measured in tangible, financial metrics, which include:

- Increase in revenue or margin;

- Reduction in costs;

- Increase in product or service creation;

- Increase in market share;

- Improvements in productivity; and

- Other metrics the company chooses.

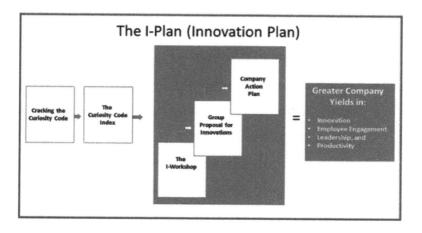

The I-Plan (Innovation Plan)

### *I-Workshops*

Innovation Workshops (or I-Workshops) and the actions that follow are the ultimate objective of this book and the CCI instrument.

Throughout the 1970s and into the twenty-first century, many companies have employed Quality Circles, Six Sigma, and similar programs that focus on improving quality through process and product development.

I-Workshops are a twenty-first-century variation of those Quality Circles and Six Sigma initiatives, but they focus on innovation. Innovations are not restricted to creating new products or technologies. They can occur in every phase of a company's operation, especially when they are strongly encouraged.

Examples include:

- Innovations in products or services
- Innovations in employee engagement
- Innovations in customer service
- Innovations in leadership
- Innovations in efficiency
- Innovations in competitiveness

I-Workshops are sanctioned by the company or division lead to empower the participants to propose the innovation of new products or practices that address key strategic issues and goals for improvement.

The workshops are conducted by an individual trained and certified in the CCI program who works with the group to find and recommend innovations in products, services, and practices on behalf of the company.

We know the power and importance of curiosity as it relates to innovation and productivity. We know that fear, assumptions, technology, and environment have the greatest influence in being able to exercise our curiosity. We know that a structured, systematic approach to analyzing and discussing those factors can lead to significant insights. And with those insights, companies can produce a plan of action that can transform their collective curiosity into improved employee engagement, decision-making, innovation, and productivity.

*Improved corporate performance and competitive advantage.* That's our #1 objective.

# Curiosity Code Index
## Findings

Name:_____     Date: _____

Company_____

**Findings**

*Fear:*_____

_____

_____

_____

*Assumptions:*_____

_____

_____

_____

*Technology:*_____

_____

_____

_____

*Environment:*_____

_____

_____

_____

*Combinations:*_____

_____

_____

_____

*Other/Notes::*_____

_____

_____

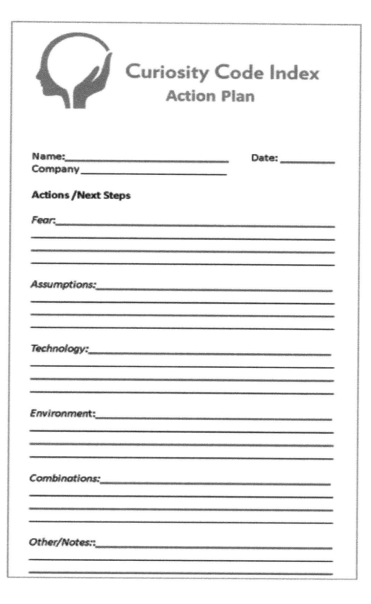

## Curiosity Code Index
### Action Plan

Name: _____     Date: _____

Company _____

**Actions /Next Steps**

*Fear:* _____

_____

_____

_____

*Assumptions:* _____

_____

_____

_____

*Technology:* _____

_____

_____

_____

*Environment:* _____

_____

_____

_____

*Combinations:* _____

_____

_____

_____

*Other/Notes::* _____

_____

_____

## Curiosity Code Index
### Corporate I-Workshop
### Recommendations and Action Plan

I-Team:_____     Date:_____

Team Members: _____

Topic::_____
_____
_____
_____

*Recommendation #1:*_____
_____
_____
_____

*Recommendation #2:*_____
_____
_____
_____

*Recommendation #3:*_____
_____
_____
_____

*Actions to Implement:*
_____
_____
_____
_____
_____
_____
_____

### *I-Workshop Follow-Up Plans and Strategies*

The output of the I-Workshop typically consists of a collection of recommended actions in the form of:

- Recommended actions related to company processes and so on;
- Recommended new products or services to explore; and
- Recommended actions regarding industry or competitive situations.

Workshop facilitators usually identify a spokesperson to report the group findings in the form of a presentation or report. In the absence of a group spokesperson, the facilitator can fill that role.

I-Workshop participants are chosen based on the assumption that they're prepared to engage in a serious undertaking of change. As such, I-Workshops are conducted only when sanctioned by the head of the company or division. It involves the understanding that the head of the organization is prepared to entertain concrete actions recommended by the workshop participants.

I-Workshops are sanctioned, arranged, and conducted on this fundamental finding:

*The best and brightest innovators, leaders, and entrepreneurs actively seek curiosity, so they willingly entertain the unfamiliar and comfortably engage the uncomfortable.*

### Facilitator's Guide

I-Workshops are conducted by a trained, certified facilitator who can be either a company designee or an outside consultant.

Facilitators are trained to:

- Administer the Curiosity Code Index;
- Conduct the I-Workshop;
- Analyze and compile the Group's results and recommendations;
- Coordinate the activities between the Group and Management; and
- Provide follow-up, as necessary.

All instructions, templates, and actions needed to implement the I-Plan are contained in a *Facilitator's Guide*, provided as part of the facilitator's training and certification process.

# *Endnotes*

1   https://www.ncbi.nlm.nih.gov/pmc/articles/PMC 3149680/

2   https://www.ncbi.nlm.nih.gov/pmc/articles/PMC 2723053/

3   https://search-proquest-com.contentproxy.phoe nix.edu/docview/1010974128?pq-origsite=summo n&accountid=166133

4   http://journals.sagepub.com.contentproxy.phoe nix.edu/doi/full/10.1177/0165025416645201?utm_ source=summon&utm_medium=discovery-pro vider

5   https://www.amazon.com/Time-Being-Annie-Dillard-ebook/dp/B003EJDGMS

6   Ibid.

7   Ibid.

8   Butler, R.A. 1957. "The influence of deprivation of visual incentives on visual exploration motivation

in monkeys." Journal of Comparative and Physio-
logical Psychology 50: 177-179.

9   Friedman, S., A. N. Nagy, and G.C. Carpenter. 1970.
    "Newborn attention: differential response decre-
    ment to visual stimuli." Journal of Experimental
    Child Psychology 10(1): 44-51.

10  https://www.amazon.com/Erik-Weihenmayer/e/
    B001ILHHJW. He was also on my show: https://
    drdianehamilton.com/vision-beyond-eyesight-
    with-erik-weihenmayer/

11  http://content.time.com/time/world/article/0,
    8599,2047596-2,00.html

12  https://www.youtube.com/watch?v=MDNSdlh
    M9cE&t=327s

13  https://en.wikipedia.org/wiki/Curiosity

14  https://www.youtube.com/watch?v=MrIWL17
    KHS0&t=16s

15  https://www.youtube.com/watch?v=V7Su2XF0To4

16  https://www.youtube.com/watch?v=MbXzVrz
    TXHQ

17  https://www.amazon.com/Drive-Surprising-
    Truth-About-Motivates/dp/1594484805

18  https://www.amazon.com/Principles-Psychology-
    William-James/dp/1855066793

19  Ibid.

20  https://www.apa.org/news/press/releases/2016/08/curiosity-behavior.aspxz

21  Ibid.

22  https://www.inc.com/julian-hayes-ii/6-habits-high-performers-use-to-stay-sharp-confident-productive-according-to-neuroscience.html

23  https://hbr.org/sponsored/2018/01/the-six-signature-traits-of-inclusive-leadership

24  https://www.forbes.com/sites/greatspeculations/2018/09/12/a-closer-look-at-netflixs-valuation/#53ce2f617bbf

25  https://www.amazon.com/Mindset-Psychology-Carol-S-Dweck/dp/0345472322

26  https://www.history.com/this-day-in-history/uss-pueblo-captured

27  https://www.amazon.com/Effective-Executive-Harvard-Business-Classics/dp/163369254X

28  https://hbr.org/2018/09/curiosity

29  https://hbr.org/2015/09/why-curious-people-are-destined-for-the-c-suite

30  Ibid.

31  Ibid.

32  https://www.amazon.com/Curious-Mind-Secret-Bigger-Life/dp/1476730776

33  https://www.amazon.com/More-Beautiful-Question-Inquiry-Breakthrough/dp/1632861054

34  https://www.amazon.com/Innovators-DNA-Mastering-Skills-Disruptive/dp/1422134814

35  https://www.amazon.com/Curious-Desire-Know-Future-Depends/dp/B00MR9RD16

36  https://hbr.org/2015/03/why-strategy-execution-unravelsand-what-to-do-about-it

37  Ibid.

38  https://www.entrepreneur.com/article/226510

39  https://www.management-issues.com/opinion/7048/leader-/

40  https://www.management-issues.com/opinion/7048/leadership-and-the-curiosity-quotient/

41  https://www.amazon.com/Loyalty-Effect-Hidden-Profits-Lasting/dp/1578516870

42  https://www.amazon.com/Building-Magnetic-Culture-Productive-Workforce-ebook/dp/B005NASHM0

43  https://www.amazon.com/1501-Reward-Employees-Nelson-Ph-D/dp/0761168788

44  https://www.amazon.com/First-Break-All-Rules-Differently-ebook/dp/B00HL2S4LW

45 https://hbr.org/2018/09/research-83-of-execu tives-say-they-encourage-curiosity-just-52-of-emp loyees-agree

46 https://en.wikipedia.org/wiki/Intelligence

47 https://www.sciencedaily.com/releases/ 2011/10/111027150211.htm

48 S. von Stumm, B. Hell, T. Chamorro-Premuzic. The Hungry Mind: Intellectual Curiosity Is the Third Pillar of Academic Performance. *Perspectives on Psychological Science,* 2011; 6 (6): 574 doi:10.1177/ 1745691611421204

49 Ibid.

50 Ibid.

51 http://pages.ucsd.edu/~nchristenfeld/Happiness_ Readings_files/Class%207%20-%20Maslow%20 1954.pdf

52 https://www.sciencedaily.com/releases/2011/ 10/111027150211.htm

53 https://www.newswire.ca/news-releases/canadian-researchers-discover-the-first-ever-link-between-intelligence-andcuriosity-538568832.html

54 https://www.amazon.com/Fred-Factor-Ordinary-Extraordinary-2004-04-20/dp/B017WQHC00

55  https://www.amazon.com/Everything-Connects-Creativity-Innovation-Sustainability/dp/0071830758

56  https://www.amazon.com/Language-Man-Learning-Speak-Creativity/dp/0983757445

57  https://www.amazon.com/Guns-Germs-Steel-Fates-Societies/dp/0393354326, p. 242.

58  http://www.destination-innovation.com/lead-and-create-by-asking-questions/

59  https://www.amazon.com/How-Think-Like-Leonardo-Vinci/dp/0440508274

60  https://www.cnbc.com/2017/11/15/warren-buffett-and-mark-cuban-agree-reading-is-key-to-success.html

61  Ibid.

62  https://hbr.org/2018/09/research-83-of-executives-say-they-encourage-curiosity-just-52-of-employees-agree

63  https://positivepsychologyprogram.com/self-actualization/

64  https://www.amazon.com/Corner-Office-Indispensable-Unexpected-Lessons/dp/1250001749

65  https://www.elizabethgilbert.com/video/

66  https://www.amazon.com/Curious-Discover-Missing-Ingredient-Fulfilling/dp/0061661198

67  Ibid.

68  Ibid.

69  https://www.huffingtonpost.com/entry/the-power-of-curiosity-to-increase-sales_us_5a57b5e6e4b0f5da618358b5

70  https://www.questia.com/library/journal/1P3-3009007551/curiosity-a-condition-for-learning

71  https://www.ncbi.nlm.nih.gov/pmc/articles/PMC5600694/

72  https://www.amazon.com/Mindset-Psychology-Carol-S-Dweck/dp/0345472322

73  https://www.ncbi.nlm.nih.gov/pmc/articles/PMC4024457/

74  https://www.azquotes.com/quote/659917

75  Journal Of Child Psychology And Psychiatry, And Allied Disciplines [J Child Psychol Psychiatry] 1972 Jun; Vol. 13 (2), pp. 121-7.

76  https://www.businessinsider.com/gen-zs-habits-different-from-millennials-2018-6

77  Ibid.

78  Ibid.

79  Gary E. Swan, The journals of gerontology. Series B, Psychological sciences and social sciences, ISSN: 1079-5014, 03/01/2002. Vol. 57, Issue 2. p.133.

80 https://report.nih.gov/nihfactsheets/ViewFact Sheet.aspx?csid=37

81 https://www.ncbi.nlm.nih.gov/pmc/articles/ PMC3578989/

82 *www.cogsci.rpi.edu/files/5065*

83 https://www.amazon.com/Shift-Your-Brilliance-Harness-Power/dp/0768404576/ref=sr_1_1?s=b ooks&ie=UTF8&qid=1541102789&sr=1-1&key words=Shift+Your+Brilliance&dpID=41chYwp %252BoPL&preST=_SY291_BO1,204,203,200_ QL40_&dpSrc=srch

84 https://www.amazon.com/Emotional-First-Aid-Rejection-Everyday/dp/0142181072/ref=sr_1_1?s= books&ie=UTF8&qid=1541102880&sr=1-1&keyw ords=emotional+first+aid+guy+winch&dpID=51 H1WKI7APL&preST=_SY344_BO1,204,203,200_ QL70_&dpSrc=srch

85 https://hbr.org/2014/08/curiosity-is-as-important-as-intelligence

86 https://www.ted.com/talks/ken_robinson_says_ schools_kill_creativity?language=en

87 https://drdianehamilton.com/sally-helgesen-and-joey-price/

88 https://drdianehamilton.com/disrupt-you-inventing-and-expanding-opportunities-with-jay-samit/

89  https://drdianehamilton.com/lolly-daskal-and-pete-winiarski/

90  https://www.lollydaskal.com/leadership/7-fears-need-overcome-effective-leader/

91  http://bit.ly/2qkK3I8

92  https://www.youtube.com/watch?v=K1SlbTZyaWE

93  https://www.amazon.com/Disrupt-You-Transformation-Opportunity-Innovation/dp/1250059372

94  https://www.amazon.com/Eat-Pray-Love-Everything-Indonesia/dp/0143038419/ref=sr_1_1?s=books&ie=UTF8&qid=1540562158&sr=1-1&keywords=eat+pray+love

95  https://www.amazon.com/Curious-Mind-Secret-Bigger-Life/dp/1476730776/ref=sr_1_1?s=books&ie=UTF8&qid=1540562273&sr=1-1&keywords=a+curious+mind+by+brian+grazer

96  http://www.nlplifetraining.com/personal-development/Curiosity-whats-it-all-about-by-Dr-Richard-Bandler

97  https://www.amazon.com/Braving-Wilderness-Quest-Belonging-Courage/dp/0812995848/ref=sr_1_2?s=books&ie=UTF8&qid=1541103233&sr=1-2&keywords=braving+the+wilderness+brene+brown+book&dpID=51RWd4PneqL&preST=_SY291_BO1,204,203,200_QL40_&dpSrc=srch

98   https://www.inc.com/peter-economy/17-brene-
     brown-quotes-to-inspire-you-to-success-and-
     happiness.html

99   https://www.youtube.com/watch?v=wMm8R6
     WJObU&t=56s

100  https://www.amazon.com/Soar-Like-Eagle-
     World-Turkeys/dp/0965476510/ref=sr_1_2?s=bo
     oks&ie=UTF8&qid=1541103660&sr=1-2&keywor
     ds=How+to+Soar+Like+an+Eagle+in+a+World+
     Full+of+Turkeys&dpID=51DJJDK1JXL&preST=_
     SY291_BO1,204,203,200_QL40_&dpSrc=srch

101  https://awfulannouncing.com/espn/jimmy-pitaro-
     espn-not-political-organization.html

102  https://www.youtube.com/watch?v=y5Rmlnok74o

103  https://www.amazon.com/Shallows-What-
     Internet-Doing-Brains/dp/0393339750/ref=sr_1_1
     ?ie=UTF8&qid=1540563099&sr=8-1&keywords=
     The+Shallows%3A+What+the+Internet+Is+Doin
     g+to+Our+Brains%2C

104  https://drdianehamilton.com/creating-disruptive-
     technology-with-jason-kintzler-and-self-manag
     ing-investments-with-randy-tate/

105  https://experts.syr.edu/en/publications/curiosity-
     interest-and-engagement-in-technology-perva
     sive-learnin

106 https://www.fastcompany.com/40440186/survey monkeys-future-is-focused-on-one-word-curiosity

107 https://www.amazon.com/Emergence-Me-Enter prise-Blueprint-Leadership/dp/1619845091/ref=sr _1_1?ie=UTF8&qid=1540563373&sr=8-1&keywo rds=Emergence+of+the+%E2%80%98Me%E2%80 %99+Enterprise

108 https://www.haydenplanetarium.org/tyson/omni bus.php/2009/07/23/called-by-the-universe

109 https://www.youtube.com/watch?v=YTE7_ fgW5WY

110 https://www.amazon.com/Hungry-Mind-Ori gins-Curiosity-Childhood/dp/0674984110/ref =sr_1_1?ie=UTF8&qid=1540563518&sr=8- 1&keywords=the+hungry+mind

111 https://www.amazon.com/Knots-R-D-Laing/ dp/0394717767